A Critique of
Max Weber's Philosophy of
Social Science

A Critique of
Max Weber's Philosophy of
Social Science

W. G. RUNCIMAN
Fellow of Trinity College, Cambridge

CAMBRIDGE
At the University Press
1972

Published by the Syndics of the Cambridge University Press
Bentley House, 200 Euston Road, London NW1 2DB
American Branch: 32 East 57th Street, New York, N.Y.10022

© Cambridge University Press 1972

Library of Congress Catalogue Card Number: 78–174257

ISBN: 0 521 08411 3

Printed in Great Britain by
Western Printing Services Limited
Bristol

PREFACE

Since this essay has been written with the English-speaking reader principally in mind, I have, where possible, given references to both the English and the German versions of Weber's writings. I have, however, modified the English version wherever this has seemed to me desirable, and the reader ought to be warned that Weber's translators cannot always be relied on. Where my own limited knowledge of German has been inadequate to resolve an uncertainty, I have sought the advice of a qualified German speaker, and I should like to express my thanks to the various friends who have helped me in this way.

Although a third edition of Weber's *Gesammelte Aufsätze zur Wissenschaftslehre* is now available published under the editorship of Johannes Winckelmann in 1968, I have continued to use the second edition of 1951, partly because it has (unlike the third edition) an index and partly because it is the one I already own. In citations of Weber's works, I have adopted the following abbreviations:

GAR   *Gesammelte Aufsätze zur Religionssoziologie*, I–III (2nd edition; Tübingen, 1922).

GASS   *Gesammelte Aufsätze zur Soziologie und Sozialpolitik* (Tübingen, 1924).

GASW   *Gesammelte Aufsätze zur Sozial- und Wirtschaftsgeschichte* (Tübingen, 1924).

GAW   *Gesammelte Aufsätze zur Wissenschaftslehre* (2nd edition; Tübingen, 1951).

GPS   *Gesammelte Politische Schriften* (2nd edition; Tübingen, 1958).

W & G   *Wirtschaft und Gesellschaft* (4th edition; Tübingen, 1956).

For English versions of selections from his works, I have adopted:

Fischoff   Ephraim Fischoff, trans., *The Sociology of Religion* (Boston, 1963).

G & M   H. H. Gerth and C. Wright Mills, eds., *From Max Weber: Essays in Sociology* (New York, 1946).

Parsons   Talcott Parsons, ed., *The Theory of Economic and Social Organization* (New York, 1947).

Parsons, *PE*   Talcott Parsons, trans., *The Protestant Ethic and the Spirit of Capitalism* (New York and London, 1930).

Rheinstein   Max Rheinstein, ed., *Max Weber on Law and Economy in Society* (Cambridge, Mass., 1954).

Shils   Edward Shils and Henry A. Finch, eds., *The Methodology of the Social Sciences* (Glencoe, Ill., 1949).

The secondary literature on Weber is by now very substantial: it has already been calculated that a bibliography on his methodology alone would contain over 600 items. Even if, therefore, it had been necessary for the purposes of this essay (which it was not) that I should deal systematically with the interpretations which have been put forward by others, I would not have attempted to do so. I have cited a number of secondary works as well as Weber's own text, but I have on the whole tried not to burden the reader with more references than are called for to enable him to see how my own interpretation has been arrived at.

I would never have written this essay at all but for a generous invitation from the Department of Social Relations at Harvard University to spend the Spring semester of 1970 there as a Visiting Lecturer on Sociology. This afforded me the benefits not only of a four-month period away from my principal, non-academic occupation, but also of the use of the unrivalled facilities of the Widener Library, and I am most grateful for it. My thanks are in addition due to Mr Anthony Quinton, who read the essay in draft and made a number of valuable comments; and to Professor Alasdair MacIntyre, Dr Aaron Sloman and Mr Alistair Young for occasional conversations to which this essay owes more than they are likely to realise. The faults which remain are entirely mine.

Finally, I should like to acknowledge my debt to Miss Catherine Tiffin for the patience and accuracy with which she typed and re-typed the manuscript.

London   W.G.R.
July 1971

I

This essay is written in the belief that it is possible to say both where Max Weber's philosophy of the social sciences is mistaken and how these mistakes can be put right. This is a bold claim; but I am more concerned to vindicate the second part of it than the first. Although it ought by now to be possible to establish a definitive interpretation of Weber's *Wissenschaftslehre* in the sense of showing both what questions he was trying to answer and what was his aim in doing so, it is not my intention to undertake the exercise here. It will be enough for my purpose if his views as I read them are in fact amenable to correction along the lines which I shall propose. Whatever disagreement there may continue to be among Weber's interpreters on points of detail, it can safely be agreed that the arguments which he put forward are fundamental to the philosophy, or if you prefer the methodology, of the social sciences. Indeed, in the half-century since Weber's death it has come to be increasingly widely held that with perhaps the sole exception of Book vi of Mill's *System of Logic* (to which Weber may have owed more than is allowed to appear in his writings) there is still no other single work of comparable importance in the academic literature on these topics. If, therefore, my attempt to correct what I hold to be Weber's mistakes is successful, this will of itself constitute at least a modest contribution to the philosophy of the social sciences. As Weber remarked à propos of Eduard Meyer, there is more to be learned from a major author who is wrong than a nonentity who is right.[1]

Weber's works are still being corrected and rearranged in successive editions, and given that he neither completed his intended writings on methodology nor set out his views on it in any systematic way it is more or less optional what should be held to constitute his contribution to *Wissenschaftslehre* as such. However, the following seven separate items can, I think, be taken effectively to make up the canon.

---

[1] *GAW*, p. 215 n1 (a note omitted by Shils). The remark recurs also in a review of Wilhelm Ostwald (*GAW*, p. 425).

1. The three connected papers, which were to have been followed by a fourth, published in *Schmollers Jahrbuch* in 1903, 1905 and 1906, under the title 'Roscher und Knies und die Logischen Probleme der Historischen Nationalökonomie: I. Roschers historische Methode. II & III. Knies und das Irrationalitätsproblem'.

2. The editorial article entitled 'Die Objektivität sozialwissenschaftlicher und sozialpolitischer Erkenntnis' published in 1904 in the *Archiv für Sozialwissenschaft und Sozialpolitik* on the occasion of the joint assumption of its editorship by Weber, Werner Sombart and Edgar Jaffé. The first section of the article is explicity stated in an opening footnote to be an agreed statement of views common to the three editors, while the second and longer section is Weber's alone.

3. The critique of Eduard Meyer published in the *Archiv* in 1906 under the title 'Kritische Studien auf dem Gebiet der Kulturwissenschaftlichen Logik: I. Zur Auseinandersätzung mit Eduard Meyer. II. Objektive Möglichkeit und adäquate Verursachung in der historischen Kausalbetrachtung'. It too was to have had a sequel, but never did.

4. The long and hostile review of the second edition of Rudolf Stammler's *Wirtschaft und Recht nach der materialistischen Geschichtsauffassung* published in the *Archiv* in 1907 under the title 'R. Stammler's "Ueberwindung" der materialistischen Geschichtsauffassung', together with a shorter supplement to it found among Weber's papers after his death.

5. The paper 'Über einige Kategorien der verstehenden Soziologie' published in *Logos* in 1913, which anticipates several of the themes of no. 7.

6. The paper 'Der Sinn der "Wertfreiheit" der soziologischen und ökonomischen Wissenschaften' which was prepared in 1913 for a closed meeting of the *Verein für Sozialpolitik* held in January 1914 and subsequently published in a revised form in *Logos* in 1918.

7. The opening sections of the posthumously published *Wirtschaft und Gesellschaft*. The third edition of the *Gesammelte Aufsätze zur Wissenschaftslehre* includes the opening seven subsections, but the most important of them for Weber's methodology is the first and longest entitled 'Begriff der Soziologie und der "Sinns" sozialen Handeln'.

Of these seven, numbers 1, 4 and 5 are still not available in

2

English. Numbers 2, 3 and 6 are available in the volume edited by Shils, and number 7 in the volume edited by Parsons; and Parsons's translation has now been incorporated in the complete translation of *Wirtschaft und Gesellschaft* published in the United States in 1968 as *Economy and Society* under the editorship of Guenther Roth and Claus Wittich. In addition, Weber's lecture given at the University of Munich in 1919 on 'Science as a Vocation', which is included in the German editions of the *Wissenschaftslehre*, is included in the selection edited by Gerth and Mills. The unavailability of numbers 1, 4 and 5, although regrettable, is not perhaps as serious as it might seem, since Weber is repetitive at many points and not only the same themes but even the same examples reappear from one part of his work to another. The lack of a complete English translation of the *Gesammelte Aufsätze zur Wissenschaftslehre* is serious; but it is, on balance, less serious than the lack of an adequate commentary.

The hazards of interpretation which Weber presents are certainly formidable. He is apt to complain, like many writers who are not only original but difficult, of being misunderstood; but the border-line between the interpretation of his views which he repudiates and the interpretation which he appears to require in its stead is often so hard to distinguish that those who have misunderstood him are scarcely to be blamed. Nor is the task made easier by the extent to which his views are developed in the course of criticising the views of others. This is not because a familiarity with the works of all the authors whom Weber criticises is a prerequisite for understanding the views of Weber himself: or if it is, then I have no business to claim an understanding of Weber. It is rather because in controverting a view which he holds to be incorrect he sometimes implies a more exaggerated counter-claim than would be consistent with what he says elsewhere. The necessary reconciliation can as a rule be effected. But the need for it in the first place is a further obstacle to the commentator who is concerned only with Weber's own view of the matter and who must be prepared, in criticising that view in its turn, to reject presuppositions which both Weber and some of his opponents may have shared.

In an essay with the purpose of this one, there is no need to go deeply into biographical detail. The circumstances of Weber's life and career no doubt explain much about both the manner and the content of his writings; but the validity of his arguments is a separate matter from their provenance. On the other hand, an exposition of Weber's views on methodology may be not merely incomplete but even misleading if it makes no reference at all to his substantive views on history and politics. The risk in a digression into these is that any apparent gains in the understanding of his methodology will be offset by an implicit involvement in the controversies by which the interpretation of his writings is, and will no doubt continue to be, beset. Weber's political views divide his commentators (particularly in Germany) even more sharply than his views on the evolution of industrial capitalism, and if an acceptable interpretation of his philosophy of social science is dependent upon an uncontroversial interpretation of his economic history, his sociology of religion, and his politics, then the chances of achieving it are slender indeed. However, it should be possible to say enough about the substantive problems by which Weber was exercised (whatever view may be taken of his solutions) to make the exposition of his methodology easier without necessarily making it more controversial. Indeed, since Weber's substantive writings are a good deal less remote from his methodological writings than some of his critics are apt to maintain, there does seem a useful purpose to be served by opening a discussion of his methodology with a summary of his work as a whole.

The range of Weber's interests was, as is well known, remarkably wide, and the influences which can be detected within it are correspondingly various. But it seems now generally accepted that the two most important individual influences were first, Marx and second, Nietzsche. The progression from the first to the second is easily discernible if one contrasts, say, the lecture which Weber delivered at Freiburg in 1896,[2] five years after his *Habilitation*, on the causes of the decline of ancient (i.e. Roman) civilisation with the lecture on 'Politics as a Vocation' which he delivered at Munich in what turned out to be the year before his death.[3] The first is Marxian not merely in substance but even in phrasing: the description of the 'signs of feudal society' as already apparent in the later empire, the reference to 'organic structural changes' occurring, and occurring of necessity, in the 'depth of society', and the interpreta-

[2] 'Die sozialen Gründe des Untergangs der antiken Kultur', in *GASW*, pp. 289–311, translated into English as 'The Social Causes of the Decay of Ancient Civilisation', *Journal of General Education* v (1950), 75–88.
[3] *GPS*, pp. 493–548 (G & M, pp. 77–128).

4

tion of the Roman economy in terms of the contradictions engendered by a mode of production resting on slavery more or less parallel the account of Marx himself. Indeed, the title of Weber's *Habilitation* dissertation – *The Agrarian History of Rome in its Significance for Public and Private Law* – reads as though directly prompted by Marx's dictum in the first volume of *Capital* that 'the secret history of the Roman republic is the history of its landed property'. The lecture on 'Politics as a Vocation', by contrast (although, unlike the companion lecture on 'Science as a Vocation', it makes no direct reference to Nietszche), betrays an unmistakable affinity to the Nietszchean idea of the 'will to power'. It was, in practice, the mixture of the two which generated the mature Weber's conception of the historical process as a struggle between 'charismatic' innovation and bureaucratic 'rationalisation' and the validity of that conception can be tested only by reference to the examples afforded by history itself.[4] But for the commentator on Weber's methodology, this conception of history makes it easier to understand his attempt to reconcile both the uniqueness and the subjective significance of historical events with the universal validity of causal laws. The manner of the reconciliation reveals the diverse and even contradictory influences of Dilthey, Menger, Rickert, Tönnies, Simmel, Troeltsch, Jellinek, Jaspers and others besides. But it would be a mistake to regard his methodology as explicable in terms of these influences alone. His substantive writings are not irrelevant to his methodology in the way that, say, Hume's *Treatise* can be considered quite independently of his *History*. A better parallel for English readers would be Collingwood: the connection may not be immediately obvious, but it would be quite mistaken to suppose that it isn't there.

This said, the sequence of Weber's principal substantive writings

---

[4] Even a cursory examination of Weber's historical writings is well beyond the scope of this essay. But it is worth remarking that just as Marx is credited in later life with the remark '*Je ne suis pas Marxiste*', so Weber is credited with a repudiation of the attempt to use the *Protestant Ethic* in support of anti-Marxism. See Paul Honigsheim, *On Max Weber* (tr. Rytina; East Lansing, 1968), p. 45: 'Hans Delbrück tried to make use of and to spread Weber's Calvinist-capitalist theory as a type of anti-Marxist idealism; Weber protested and told me, "I really must object to this; I am much more materialistic than Delbrück thinks"'; and cf. *GAW*, p. 169 (Shils, p. 71), *GAW*, p. 295, *GAR* I, 205–6 (Parsons, *PE*, p. 183) and *W & G* I, 349 (Fischoff, p. 208).

may be shortly summarised. Given the length and the seriousness of the nervous breakdown (or however it should be described)[5] which interrupted his career, his writings fall into two distinct periods. The first of these ends in 1897 when he moved from his first professorship at Freiburg to take Knies's chair at Heidelberg (and when, for what significance it may have, his father died); the second opens with his acceptance of the co-editorship of the *Archiv für Sozialwissenschaft und Sozialpolitik* in 1903, his visit to the United States in 1904, and the publication not only of the critique of Roscher and of the two articles on *The Protestant Ethic and the Spirit of Capitalism* but also of articles on the system of land tenure in Prussia and the social structure of ancient Germany.[6] If we leave aside his doctoral dissertation on the mediaeval trading companies, published in 1889, the writings of the first period are concerned with three different but related themes: the legal and economic history of Rome, the stock exchange, and the economic policies of the Junkers in their estates to the East of the Elbe. In 1895, following his appointment at Freiburg, he delivered an Inaugural Lecture on the political economy of East Prussia which is remarkable (and was so regarded at the time) for its outspoken support of a doctrine of *Realpolitik* and advocacy of a policy of German national interest; and it has for this reason an ironic interest for the critic of his later methodology, since it is an example of precisely what he was to deplore in other occupants of university chairs.[7] Yet whatever their

---

[5] There is enough evidence on Weber's symptoms to provide scope for psychiatric conjecture, but not enough for any definitive diagnosis. Weber wrote an account of his symptoms himself which Marianne Weber passed to Jaspers, and Jaspers subsequently described to Eduard Baumgarten as unique in its objectivity and clarity. But under Hitler, Jaspers returned the manuscript to Marianne for fear that it would not be safe either in his own house or in a library, and she destroyed it during the Second World War for the same reason. See Eduard Baumgarten, *Max Weber: Werk und Person* (Tübingen, 1964), pp. 641–2.

[6] 'Agrarstatistische und sozialpolitische Betrachtungen zur Fideikommissfrage in Preussen', in *GASS*, pp. 323–93; and 'Der Streit um den charakter der altgermanischen Sozialverfassung in der deutschen Literatur des letzten Jahrzents', in *GASW*, pp. 508–56.

[7] The lecture, which was entitled 'Der Nationalstaat und die Volkswirtschaftspolitik', is reprinted in *GPS*, pp. 1–25. Weber did, despite his later advocacy of value-free social science, continue to use his influence where he could in matters of social policy. In 1912, indeed, he called a meeting of the reformist members of the *Verein für Sozialpolitik* to plan a public meeting in Frankfurt to found a new organisation explicitly dedicated to social reform – a project torpedoed only by Brentano's refusal to parti-

significance in the light of what was to follow them, the writings of Weber's first period would not, in the opinion of any commentator known to me, have by themselves earned him a reputation even distantly comparable to the reputation earned him by his subsequent work. By the time that he emerged from his illness, however, the ideas for which he is now celebrated seem to have been more or less fully formed. He did not abandon his earlier interests: not only do they recur at numerous points in his later work, but he wrote a substantially extended version of an earlier essay of 1897 on the economic history of the ancient world for the third edition of the *Handwörterbuch der Staatswissenschaften* which was published in 1909.[8] But whereas he could have been described in the earlier period as a legal historian and political economist, however unusually learned in the social and economic history of both the ancient and the modern world, the label is increasingly inadequate in the later. The time which he spent in Italy during his illness had helped to give him an interest in the history of art which is reflected to advantage in his methodological as well as his substantive writings; the *Protestant Ethic* was in due course followed by the series of essays on Confucianism and Taoism, Hinduism and Buddhism, and ancient Judaism;[9] an abortive enquiry instituted by the *Verein* into the determinants of industrial workers' output took him for a short period into industrial psychology and empirical survey analysis;[10] his interest in the progressive 'rationalisation' of Western art led to an essay published only after his death on the

cipate unless Social Democrats were included, which led to a permanent breach between Brentano and Weber (see James J. Sheehan, *The Career of Lujo Brentano* [Chicago, 1966], p. 175). But this is not inconsistent with his subsequent stand at the *Verein*'s debate on values: as he had already written in the editorial of 1904, scientific objectivity and lack of personal convictions are quite separate matters (*GAW*, p. 157 (Shils, p. 60)).

[8] 'Agrarverhältnisse im Altertum', in *GASW*, pp. 1–288.

[9] These three essays first appeared in the *Archiv für Sozialwissenschaft und Sozialpolitik* between 1916 and 1918, and were reprinted in the three volumes of *GAR*. They have been made available in English as *The Religion of China* (tr. Gerth; New York, 1951), *The Religion of India* (tr. Gerth and Martindale; New York, 1958) and *Ancient Judaism* (tr. Gerth and Martindale; New York, 1952). Translations from the 'Einleitung' and 'Zwischenbetrachtung' are available in G & M, chs. XI and XIII.

[10] See 'Methodologische Einleitung für die Erhebungen des Vereins für Sozialpolitik über Auslese und Anpassung (Berufswahl und Berufsschicksal) der Arbeiterschaft der geschlossene Grossindustrie' and 'Zur Psychophysik der industriellen Arbeit', in *GASS*, pp. 1–60, 61–255.

sociology of music;[11] and the monumental but uncompleted *Economy and Society* contains a sufficient wealth at once of typological analysis, comparative generalisation and straightforward economic and social history to earn for him by itself a place among the classics of European social theory.[12] Even this list omits his less strictly academic writings, which include articles on the politics of Germany and Russia,[13] as well as the companion lectures of 1919 on 'Politics as a Vocation' and 'Science as a Vocation'. It can all too often be said of writers on the philosophy of social science that they are preaching about subjects which they have never practised; but against none could the charge be less appropriately levelled than Weber.

Given this remarkable succession of writings, it is of course an oversimplification to treat Weber's views as though all of them were derived from a unitary, preconceived body of doctrine. Even if, as I have suggested, his principal ideas are recognisable as early as the *Protestant Ethic* and the critique of Knies (if not of Roscher), there could hardly fail to be some modification and development of them over the period. *Economy and Society*, in particular, although it contains much that can be found in his earlier writings, also contains much on questions both of method and of substance that cannot. But for the purpose of this essay, I think it is legitimate to treat his methodological writings, unsystematic though they may be, as a more or less coherent whole. Whatever the difficulties which they present, and whatever the changes in emphasis and style between the involved and laborious critique of Knies and the authoritative and systematic exposition of the meaning of social action which opens *Economy and Society*, Weber is not one of

---

[11] It was first published in 1921, and is translated into English as *The Rational and Social Foundations of Music* (tr. Martindale, Riedel and Neuwirth; Carbondale, Ill., 1958).

[12] In 1923, the year after the publication of *Economy and Society*, there was also published a version of the lectures which Weber delivered at Munich in 1919–20 on economic history, based on the notebooks of students who had attended them. It was published in English in 1927 under the title *General Economic History* (trans. F. H. Knight) but without the German editors' *Begriffliche Vorbemerkungen*. Its value for the study of Weber's methodology is at best marginal.

[13] The most important of the political articles are 'Wahlrecht und Demokratie in Deutschland' (*GPS*, pp. 233–79), 'Parlament und Regierung im neugeordneten Deutschland' (*GPS*, pp. 294–431), and a lecture delivered to an audience of Austrian officers in Vienna in 1918 on 'Der Sozialismus' (*GASS*, pp. 492–518).

those authors who keeps changing his mind or whose views as expressed in one part of his work are fundamentally at odds with his views as expressed in another. The methodological writings when taken together are by no means free of inconsistencies. But this, I believe, is almost always because they contain what might be called authentic confusions, which are if anything made easier to diagnose if they are consistently maintained.

The more difficult problem by which Weber's interpreters are faced is that much of his writing on methodology is not only so polemical but at the same time so very eclectic. It is accordingly difficult not only, as I have already remarked, accurately to sift out Weber's own views but also to detect just how far the authors whom he cites did or did not in fact elicit his agreement. He refers freely to many of his predecessors and contemporaries, including all those whom I have so far named. But the reader is left with the suspicion that some of these references suggest more, and others less, affinity than was in fact the case. Thus Weber's references to Rickert, for example, seem in part to have been dictated by politeness to a family friend: it is clearly unwarranted to speak of him, as one American commentator has done, as Weber's 'philosophical master'.[14] His references to Simmel, by contrast, frequent though they are, almost certainly underestimate the debt which he owed to him. Although the term 'ideal type' came from Jellinek and not from Simmel, the idea behind it, in the form which Weber was to adopt, probably came to him from Simmel's *Philosophy of Money*, of which Weber's personal copy survives, as does his copy of Simmel's *Schopenhauer and Nietszche*, with numerous annotations in his own hand.[15]

It is even possible that the total lack of any reference to Durkheim, whom Weber's present-day commentators are likely to agree to be the most important of his contemporaries, should be read as a deliberate and therefore significant refusal of mention. There was

[14] H. Stuart Hughes, *Consciousness and Society: the Reorientation of European Social Thought 1890–1930* (New York, 1958), p. 309. Contrast Eugène Fleischmann, De Weber à Nietzsche', *Archives Européennes de Sociologie* v (1964), 198–201, citing the testimony of Troeltsch's *Der Historismus und Seine Probleme*, published in 1922.
[15] See Friedrich H. Tenbruck, 'Die Genesis der Methodologie Max Webers', *Kölner Zeitschrift fur Soziologie* xi (1959), 620–4. That the actual term 'ideal type' came from Jellinek is attested by Marianne Weber, *Max Weber: ein Lebensbild* (Tübingen, 1926), p. 327; but see further Fleischmann, *op. cit.* p. 199 n37.

no reason for them ever to have met, since when Weber visited Paris from Heidelberg in the summer of 1911 it was purely for pleasure and when Durkheim visited Germany in 1886 Weber was still three years away from his doctorate. But when Durkheim's nephew and collaborator Marcel Mauss visited Weber at Heidelberg he saw a complete set of *L'Année Sociologique* on his shelves;[16] and Weber must in any case have known something of Durkheim's work through Simmel, who was listed on the title-page of the first (although only the first) volume of *L'Année* as an editorial collaborator, and even contributed an article to it. What is more, there is at least one passage in *Economy and Society* which reads almost unmistakably as an indirect reference to Durkheim: in the opening passage of the section on the sociology of religion Weber refers (in order to dismiss it) to the view that magic is to be distinguished from religion by the fact that priests do, and magicians don't, have an institutional affiliation, and it is hard to know who he could have been thinking of if it wasn't Durkheim.[17] It might even not be wholly fanciful to suggest a connection between Weber's animus against Stammler's *Wirtschaft und Recht* and the very favourable review of the first edition by François Simiand in the first volume of *L'Année*.

Not too much should, however, be made of all this, since no definite evidence will ever be forthcoming. It has been remarked that *L'Année* under Durkheim's editorship contained only the most fleeting references to Weber while Durkheim himself wrote an unfavourable review of the book on the 'Woman Question' published by Weber's wife, Marianne, in 1907.[18] But Marianne's book dealt with a subject in which Durkheim was genuinely interested, whereas Weber himself never wrote a *book* which *L'Année* should have been expected to review: the *Protestant Ethic*, after all, first consisted of two journal articles, and *L'Année* briefly noticed them both – the second very favourably. The question of Weber's attitude to Durkheim is relevant to the interpretation of his methodology only because it might perhaps be justifiable to read Weber as im-

---

[16] See Raymond Aron, *Main Currents in Sociological Thought* (tr. Howard and Weaver; London, 1968), II, 224, to whom this was reported by Mauss himself.

[17] *W & G* I, 259–60 (Fischoff, pp. 28–9).

[18] Edward A. Tiryakian, 'A Problem for the Sociology of Knowledge', *Archives Européennes de Sociologie* VII (1966), 334.

plicitly concerned on one topic, at least, to counter Durkheim's views.

It is commonly said of Weber that he was fighting a war on two fronts, against the extremes of Idealism on one side and Positivism on the other; but it ought not to be forgotten that he was at the same time fighting a related campaign, again on two fronts, where his opponents were the two extremes of Holism and Psychologism. Weber was what is nowadays called a 'methodological individualist'. Just as he was concerned to reject the extravagances of neo-Kantianism, whether in the style of Dilthey or of Rickert, without falling back into the arms of those who wished to deny all difference of kind between the social and the natural sciences, so he was concerned to reject any hint of reification of collective concepts without falling back into the arms of those who would unreservedly assimilate sociology to psychology. There is extant a letter written in the last few months of his life in which he goes so far as to say that his reason for being a sociologist at all is to put an end to the influence of collective concepts by which the subject continues to be haunted;[19] and although this may not in fact have been an implicit reference to Durkheim (since it could, after all, apply merely to the German 'organicists') the latter-day commentator must be tempted to remark that even if it isn't, it might as well be. To invoke Durkheim as Weber's notional opponent makes it easier to disentangle some of the strands which are almost inextricably intertwined in Weber's criticisms of his philosophical and socio-logical compatriots. Admittedly, it is for the very reason that they were so intertwined that Weber's distinctive compromise is so valuable. But it is important to remember that there is no necessary logical connection between Idealism and Holism on the one hand or between Positivism and Individualism on the other. Durkheim was both Positivist and Holist; and whatever may be said against Durkheim's own *Rules of Sociological Method*, it might turn out that something more of Positivism should be retained than Weber was willing to do without affecting one way or the other his position on the debate between Individualism in the manner of Mill and Holism in the manner of Durkheim.

The entanglement of ostensibly related doctrines is further

[19] Weber to Robert Liefmann, 9 March 1920, quoted by Wolfgang Mommsen, 'Max Weber's Political Sociology and his Philosophy of World History', *International Social Science Journal* XVII (1965), p. 44 n2.

complicated by the simultaneous arguments which were equally popular among Weber's contemporaries over the demarcations within the sciences as a whole, and particularly the demarcation between the sciences of '*Geist*' or '*Kultur*' and the sciences of nature. This might seem, at first sight, a distinction which could be predicted to be argued along the lines of the Idealist/Positivist, even if not of the Holist/Individualist dispute. But the Idealists were divided on it. Where Dilthey had distinguished the *Geisteswissenschaften* in terms of subject-matter, Windelband and Rickert distinguished *Geschichtswissenschaft* in terms of method: in the vocabulary which we owe to Windelband, the 'historical' sciences are not 'nomothetic' but 'idiographic'. The boundaries which the two schools wished to draw were therefore quite different, and it was possible for two disputants to agree that there *is* a boundary while disagreeing whether the social sciences are to be distinguished from the natural because the former do, but the latter do not, seek to explain human thought and culture or because the former cannot, but the latter can, proffer well-tested explanations in terms of general laws. Once again, there is no necessary logical connection. History may proffer successful explanations by reference to general laws although it deals with what goes on in the human mind just as natural science may include historical explanations of an 'idiographic' kind. Weber's position, to be sure, was not that of Windelband any more than that of Rickert or Dilthey. But he did distinguish sociology – a term which in general he disliked – from history on the grounds that the historian does not try to construct 'type concepts' or formulate 'general rules' whereas the sociologist does.[20] There is nothing wrong with this distinction if it is a useful one,

[20] The contrast is drawn in *GAW*, p. 545 (Parsons, p. 109). For Weber's dislike of the term, see his remark about '*eine Gesellschaft mit diesem bei uns unpopulären Namen*' in his address at the first meeting of the German Sociological Association in 1910 (*GASS*, p. 431); and Jaspers's testimony that 'He was opposed to the establishment of professorships in sociology' (*Three Essays: Leonardo, Descartes, Max Weber* [tr. Manheim; New York, 1953], p. 247). It has been persuasively argued by Emerich Francis, 'Kultur und Gesellschaft in der Soziologie Max Webers', in Karl Engisch et al., eds., *Max Weber: Gedächtnisschrift der Ludwig-Maximilians-Universität München* (Berlin, 1966), pp. 89–114, that Weber's writings show a progressive shift away from the notion of *Kulturwissenschaft* and towards that of *Soziologie*. But it may be significant that even so Weber describes himself in 'Science as a Vocation' as a 'political economist' (*GAW*, p. 566 (G & M, p. 129); and cf. the reference to 'sociologists' at p. 572 (G & M, p. 134)), while even the letter to Liefmann (above, n. 19)

whether analytically or descriptively. But it does leave open the possibility that from the standpoint of the logic of explanation the difference might be less important than it seemed three-quarters of a century ago.

Descriptively, the difference is clear enough. The German historians of Weber's youth didn't generalise, although they were self-consciously scientific; and conversely the psychologists, who did generalise, were responsible in Weber's eyes for pushing the gap between 'subjective' and 'objective' altogether too wide. But their variations of practice as well as of doctrine made it remarkably difficult (as it is to this day) to formulate precisely the fundamental problems of the philosophy of the social sciences and to find adequate labels to characterise the views of the rival individuals or schools among which a choice, if reconciliation is impossible, needs to be made. I have talked about Idealists and Positivists; but these terms can cover several mutually incompatible viewpoints even apart from the differences with which they may or may not coincide on the separate questions of methodological individualism and the demarcation of natural from social science. Despite their imprecision, and more specifically the differences between self-styled 'Positivists' and self-styled 'Naturalists', I shall continue in this essay to use these terms because it is still useful to have some sort of label to distinguish those who do from those who don't believe that there is some fundamental difference in kind between the physical and biological sciences on one side and the sciences of human behaviour on the other. But I had better emphasise that they are labels of convenience only. It would undo all the purpose of what I have said about the difficulty of extracting Weber's arguments from their polemical context if I were then to categorise them in terms as misleading as any that either he or his adversaries used.

One final preliminary point remains to be made. Despite what I have said about the connection between Weber's methodological and substantive writings, I propose to ignore the one topic on which his ideas most obviously furnish this connection – his typology of action. As we shall see, Weber believed that the terms in which sociological explanations must be couched are terms which classify the self-conscious actions of persons responsive to the

hardly betrays an unequivocal acceptance of the title 'sociologist'. (Incidentally, too, Francis misprints [p. 103] Weber's remark at the 1910 congress as '*diesem bei uns populären Namen*'.)

actions of other persons by reference to the motives which can be ascribed to them. It follows that we should expect him to propose some general classification of human action according to motive; and this is just what he does in distinguishing 'affectual', 'traditional', 'value-rational' and 'purpose-rational' action. Much critical attention has been given to this classification. But my reason for ignoring it is simply that it raises more difficulties than it solves. Whatever its rationale, Weber's classification of action cannot be rescued, even if drastically modified, from the objections which have been levelled against it. The distinction between 'value-rationality' and 'purpose-rationality', to which corresponds the distinction more common among English-speaking sociologists between 'expressive' and 'instrumental' action, continues to be widely used. But it can as well be expressed in terms of the traditional distinction between means and ends, and since the traditional distinction involves no ambiguities which are not inherent in Weber's formulation also, it seems more sensible to revert to the traditional distinction. In so doing, I have no wish necessarily to deny that a general classification of motives may be necessary to the explanation of the social behaviour of human beings; that Weber's use of the term 'rationalisation' to describe the fundamental process which he saw at work in Western society may be both legitimate and informative; or that 'rationality' may not be capable of precise formulation within certain definable categories of human actions and the decisions which precede them. My wish is simply to avoid the risk that by failing to discard without compunction one of the more vulnerable of Weber's doctrines I might weaken my claims on behalf of those others that seem to me to be of more lasting interest.

14

II

Since I shall be arguing that Weber was (however instructively) mistaken, it may be as well if I specify at the outset where I believe his mistakes to lie. Summarily put, Weber was wrong on three issues: the difference between theoretical presuppositions and implicit value-judgements; the manner in which 'idiographic' explanations are to be subsumed under causal laws; and the relation of explanation to description. If this were all that needed to be said, a detailed critique of his doctrines would no doubt be of merely antiquarian interest. But not only does he advance a number of arguments which are entirely sound; he is also right in the terms in which he asks the questions to which these arguments afford a part of the answer. In the first place, he is right to try to show what, if anything, still differentiates the sciences of man from the sciences of nature once we have accepted the universal validity of the criteria of science. Second, he is right to devote his attention to the four most plausible candidates: the potential intrusion of value-judgements; the subjective nature of social action; the uniqueness of historical events; and the irreducibility (or not) of sociology to psychology. The decisive difference between the sciences of man and nature may not be quite what Weber thought. But if nothing else, it is hardly deniable that these questions do call for resolution in the sciences of man in a way that doesn't arise in the first place in the sciences of nature.

Once the problem has been put in these terms, it can equally well be approached from either end. Those who hold that there is still no fundamental difference (whatever 'fundamental' may mean) between the natural and the social sciences will approach it by asking why there should be thought to be such a difference and setting out to discredit whichever of the four candidates is then put forward. Those who hold that social-scientific explanation proceeds by some quite other method and even, perhaps, appeals to some other criterion of validation will approach it by showing how inappropriate to human behaviour are the methods of the natural sciences and expounding the contrasting method by which alone (on their

15

view) successful explanation of what people think and do can be attained. These two approaches are not exhaustive. It is, after all, possible to argue that human action isn't explicable at all. But this sort of radical scepticism derives from metaphysical considerations by which few practitioners of social science in any of its various forms are, or need to be, disquieted. Weber never takes it seriously: it appears in his writings only once – and then indirectly – when in a passage in the third part of the essay on Roscher and Knies he dismisses Croce's view that since history cannot be directly known the historian must proceed by artistic intuition.[21] It is a fundamental assumption of Weber's that sociology is a matter of discovery, not of invention. It is true that this does not of itself place him among those who approach the problem from the Positivists' end, because he is consistently at pains to emphasise, even when attacking what he regards as the aberrations of 'Hegelian Emanatism', that the criterion of validation common to the natural and the social scientist neither presupposes nor requires a common procedure. On the other hand, it would be still more inappropriate to read him as concerned to expound some alternative form of modified Idealism, since most of his criticisms are directed against those who so exaggerate the differences which they detect that they thereby remove the explanation of human action from the realm of science altogether. Weber's position, therefore, should be construed as a self-conscious and deliberate attempt to have it both ways. He agrees with the Positivists that the social sciences are value-free and causal. But he denies that this agreement is incompatible with the view that there is nevertheless a difference of kind between the sciences of nature and the sciences of man. Or to look at it the other way round: he acknowledges the peculiarities of human social behaviour as a subject for science, but believes it possible to allow for them without compromising scientific method.

In any discussion of the philosophy of the social sciences, the course of the argument is likely to be dictated by the examples chosen to the intended advantage of one or the other side. Not that any single example will ever prove whether and in what way explanation in the sciences of man is different from explanation in the sciences of nature; but the readiest test of either the strict Positivist or the strict Idealist case is to try it out on an example deliberately chosen for its difficulties. To the Idealist, who regards

[21] *GAW*, p. 108.

16

with suspicion and even incredulity the suggestion that the social sciences should proceed according to the 'deductive-nomological' model of natural-scientific method, the best rejoinder is to ask how else he would set out to establish and justify, say, an explanation of the sixteenth-century European price-rise. But to the Positivist, who takes the appropriateness of the deductive-nomological model for granted, the best rejoinder is to ask how he proposes to explain (to take one of Weber's own favourite examples) Goethe's *Faust*. Now since Weber's own position rests on the explicit recognition that both sides are partly correct and partly mistaken, it is rather difficult to decide which sort of example to choose for the purpose of expounding and criticising his views. But the best way, I think, is to treat him as someone who looks more of an Idealist than in fact he is, and to show how his view that the concept of motive is essential to social-scientific explanation is still compatible with an unwavering belief in the unity of science. Accordingly, I shall take as a first example the topic which is in general the most likely to raise difficulties for the Positivist case: the history of art.

Since I am arguing that it would be even more inaccurate to classify Weber as an Idealist rather than a Positivist, it may be as well to cite at once his insistence that ideas are conditioned by psychology, not by logic; that mental and cultural events are no less 'objectively' governed by laws than any other events; and that human action is not less explicable – indeed it is more so – when it follows from the self-conscious pursuit by the most effective means of a freely chosen end.[22] But despite all this, it is (he argues) foolish to suggest that the unique configurations of cultural phenomena with which the art historian deals, whether individual works like the Sistine Madonna or styles and periods like the Gothic, can be explained by derivation from general laws and the kinds of concepts appropriate to them. He never sets out in detail the model of natural-scientific explanation with which he contrasts the procedures of the sociologist or historian. The terms which he uses, however, are those of the so-called 'Naturalism' of his period; and it seems fairly clear that what he has in mind is the sort of paradigm which is to be found in any number of present-day texts in the

[22] *GAW*, pp. 198 (Shils, p. 96), 180 (Shils, p. 80) and 226–7 (Shils, pp. 124–5). On the last point, Weber himself footnotes a reference to the critique of Roscher and Knies where, as he says, the error in question is 'exhaustively criticised'.

philosophy of science. Scientific explanation, as it continues generally to be conceived, renders the *explanandum* predictable in principle by identifying it as one of a class of states or events whose occurrence either necessarily or with a specified probability follows from the conjunction of observable initial conditions and at least one relevant general law. In a familiar example from Ernest Nagel, the formation of moisture on the surface of a glass of cold water at a given time and place is explained in terms of a statement of initial conditions which specifies the difference of temperature and a general law about condensation.[23] But how could we ever fit the Sistine Madonna to this paradigm? A possible answer might be to say that it is just a matter of waiting for sociology to discover the appropriate laws. But one need not accept the premises of the Idealists in order to agree with Weber that there is something unsatisfying about such a suggestion. In the first place, we are dealing with an explanandum which as a work of art belongs in a category peculiar to itself, just as will the books and paintings of future ages which these undiscovered laws would supposedly enable us to predict. In the second place, what the art historian actually does is something quite different – he seeks to understand the work in terms of the artist's own intentions and ideas, he selects (or indeed coins) what he then regards as the concepts appropriate to describe it, and only finally does he turn to the generalisations of psychology (or any other science which may offer relevant generalisations to him) as one possible means among several for helping him to establish a definitive account of why the Sistine Madonna came to be painted as and when it was. Weber even goes so far as to say that in the 'cultural sciences' knowledge of the general is never of value in itself. This may seem a little extreme: indeed, this is one of the instances where what Weber says in one place is inconsistent, if taken at face value, with what he says in another.[24] But it is certainly true, as the anti-Positivists have not failed to remind us, that

[23] Ernest Nagel, *The Structure of Science* (London, 1961), pp. 30–2.
[24] The statement is made in the 1904 editorial (*GAW*, p. 180 (Shils, p. 80)), where Weber is arguing that in the *Kulturwissenschaften* the most general laws are the least useful in practice. But by the time he wrote the opening sections of *Economy and Society*, he was at any rate prepared (in the same passage which I have already cited) to talk of sociology as a 'generalising science capable of contributing to causal historical explanation': see *GAW*, pp. 545–6 (Parsons, p. 109), and cf. *W & G* I, 194 (Rheinstein, p. 33) where sociology is described as a discipline 'seeking empirical regularities'.

whereas in a developed natural science we attach greater credence to general laws than to particular facts which if accepted would disconfirm them, in history we attach greater credence to particular facts than to the general hypotheses from which they could in theory be derived;[25] and Weber continued to hold, even in his latest writings, that the quest for empirical generalisations is only an adjunct or preliminary to a fully satisfying historical explanation of self-conscious human conduct.

Now this scepticism of Weber's about the possibility of general laws of human behaviour is likely to remind English readers of the view later expounded by Collingwood. Indeed, readers familiar with Collingwood's autobiography may already have called to mind the engaging passage in which Collingwood traces his first realisation of the distinctive nature of historical explanation to his inability to understand what could possibly have been in the minds of those responsible for the construction of the Albert Memorial.[26] Collingwood's emphasis on the historian's need to see things as his subjects saw them, his insistence that history is concerned with acts as explicitly distinguished from events, and even his view that classical economics 'can do no more than describe in a general way certain characteristics of the historical age in which it is constructed'[27] are all reminiscent of the arguments advanced by Weber in the editorial of 1904. But the difference lies in the one decisive error which Collingwood commits but Weber avoids. I don't mean by this the untestable appeal to some purely whimsical intuition, because this interpretation of Collingwood, although by no means uncommon, can be maintained (as in Weber's case) only at a safe distance from the actual text of his writings. I mean instead his deliberate conflation of explanation and understanding. Collingwood and those like him who have claimed that history is an account of the thoughts, motives and ideas of historical persons are claiming nothing paradoxical if they are understood merely to mean that since the actions which historians wish to explain are indeed actions and not simply reflexes, an adequate history must specify by what

---

[25] See Isaiah Berlin, 'The Concept of Scientific History', in William H. Dray, ed., *Philosophical Analysis and History* (New York, 1966), pp. 14–17.

[26] R. G. Collingwood, *An Autobiography* (Oxford, 1939), ch. 5.

[27] Collingwood, *The Idea of History* (Oxford, 1946), p. 224. Compare *GAW*, pp. 176–7 (Shils, p. 77) on the impossibility of deriving the 'cultural significance' of a monetary economy from any economic 'law'.

thoughts, motives and ideas those actions were preceded or con-stituted. How, after all, can the social scientist claim to account for anyone's beliefs and actions without establishing in the course of his investigation what those beliefs and actions actually *were*? And how can he do this without in some quite innocuous metaphorical sense 'entering into' the minds of the people in question? The error to which this can lead, however, is to suppose that explanation comes to an end when this has been done. It is not simply that an explanation which purports to derive from this sort of understand-ing must, as Weber requires, be tested against evidence which is intersubjectively accessible to any competent observer. In addition, the investigator must ask himself how his subjects came to have the thoughts and therewith perform the actions which he has succeeded in identifying. It is only in one very limited sense true that (to borrow a slightly different example from a still more recent author in the Idealist tradition) 'to know that a priest is celebrating mass is, in general, to know why he is doing it'.[28] This is merely another way of saying that to know *that* a priest is celebrating mass is to know *what* he is doing in talking and gesturing in this fashion: the investigator has both to have understood what 'celebrating mass' means and to have established that the priest whom he observes is 'really' doing it (and not for some reason merely offering a simula-tion of what it *would* look like if he *were* 'really' doing it). This can admittedly be a difficult matter which in the case of an alien culture will require training and skill on the researcher's part. But this is no reason whatever for claiming that it is then unnecessary, let alone meaningless, to go on to ask why the priest *is* celebrating mass. Indeed, if the suggestion were taken literally it would lead to the bizarre conclusion that the only answer which the historian, anthropologist or sociologist can give to the question 'Why is he celebrating mass?' is 'Don't you see? He is *celebrating mass*'.

Examples of this kind have often been cited by anti-Positivist philosophers to support a claim that the distinctiveness of human action, and therefore of the explanations appropriate to it, lies in the fact that it is governed by a conscious recognition of rules. But

[28] A. R. Louch, *Explanation and Human Action* (Oxford, 1966), p. 163. Collingwood, it ought to be said, repudiates the label 'Idealist' as vehe-mently as Popper, for example, repudiates the label 'Positivist'; but since I am using these only as labels of convenience I hope I may be forgiven. 'Idealism' does not have to stand only for the doctrines of Hegel any more than 'Positivism' only for those of the Vienna Circle.

Weber, who devoted a long section of his critique of Stammler to the notion of 'following a rule', uses it rather to draw the Positivists' conclusion. His discussion has an added interest in view of the attention which has been given to the notion of 'following a rule' in recent Anglo-American philosophy, largely under the influence of the *Philosophical Investigations* of Wittgenstein. But the only English-speaking commentator who has, as far as I know, drawn attention to its importance uses it to argue that Weber ought to, but doesn't, take it to the fundamentally Idealist conclusion implicit in his doctrine of 'understanding'.[29] Weber's own intention is, however, very different. He embarks on the discussion chiefly in order to expose three particular confusions which he detects, among others, in Stammler: first, between moral rules and legal rules; second, between legal and/or moral rules and empirical regularities of behaviour; third, between regularities of behaviour deriving from law and regularities deriving from custom. He is admittedly concerned to make clear the importance of the concept of a rule to that of meaningful action: in the example which he gives, a slip of paper inserted between the pages of a book is a 'bookmark' only because of the intended subsequent action which it implies.[30] But the moral which Weber argues from the whole discussion, and illustrates with a succession of examples of the role of 'rules' in human conduct, including the rules of a game, is that the explanation of conduct cannot be inferred by simple reference to the rules appropriate to the standard case. Rules, according to Weber, enter into the empirical study of actual rule-governed behaviour in three logically distinct ways: as constituting the activity itself and the concepts which describe it; as 'heuristically' implying a mode of, and thus a potential hypothesis about, the activity; and as of themselves furnishing a putative cause of some aspects of the activity observed.[31] But in every case, the explanation of the behaviour in

[29] Peter Winch, *The Idea of a Social Science* (London, 1958), pp. 49–51, 116–120. Independent testimony that this was the opposite of Weber's intentions is furnished by the article written after Weber's death by Rickert, who had every reason to assimilate Weber's doctrines to his own but conceded none the less that any thought of treating sociology like philosophy was remote from Weber's ideas: see Heinrich Rickert, 'Max Weber und seine Stellung zur Wissenschaft', *Logos* xv (1926), 228.
[30] *GAW*, p. 332.
[31] *GAW*, p. 342. The distinction between constitutive and regulative rules, which had been foreshadowed by Kant in the 'Appendix to the Transcendental Dialectic. Of the Regulative Use of the Ideas of Pure Reason' in

question requires an empirically testable account of its causes, and it is an empirical question, not a logical one, what part the rules of it have to play in this account. The fact that the rules must be understood if we are to understand the meaning of the actions observed to the agents themselves does not absolve us from an empirical demonstration of how it comes about that the rules are (or are not) followed in practice.

This applies, on Weber's view, to the rules of arithmetic no less than the rules of a card game. It is true that to the observer, as to most if not all of those whom he observes, the rules of arithmetic and more generally of logic have a unique validity. But the hypothesis that a person's behaviour is to some degree to be explained by his following of those rules stands or falls irrespective of their epistemological status in the observer's eyes. Not only is it possible for a person to display a consistent pattern of behaviour which is not in fact the result of his conscious adherence to a normative rule even though it is outwardly identical with the behaviour which would result from such adherence; it is also possible for a pattern of behaviour to result from adherence to rules which the observer knows to be incorrect. Weber gives the example, drawn from one of his own fields of study, of the Pythagorean theory of music: we know that twelve fifths are not in fact the equivalent of seven octaves, but the Pythagorean theory can be explained only by recognising that it is based on this erroneous calculation.[32] In such cases, the model of 'rational' calculation merely furnishes a sort of stalking-horse whose function for the empirical investigator is the same as the model of 'rational' behaviour in classical economics. He will deduce from a deliberately fictional model what *would* be the behaviour he would observe *if* the people in question were to act in accordance with the specified set of rules; but if he is to

the *Critique of Pure Reason*, has also received a good deal of attention in recent English-speaking philosophy: see e.g. J. R. Searle, 'How to Derive "Ought" from "Is"', in W. D. Hudson, ed., *The Is-Ought Question* (London, 1969), p. 131, where Kant's distinction is acknowledged and the related distinction drawn by John Rawls, 'Two Concepts of Rules', *Philosophical Review* LXIV (1955), pp. 3–32, is cited also. Weber's own views on Kant seem to have been influenced not, as they might have been, by the Marburg School of Hermann Cohen so much as by Windelband's *History of Philosophy*, whose chapter on Kant in Weber's copy is, according to Dieter Henrich, *Die Einheit der Wissenschaftslehre Max Webers* (Tübingen, 1952), p. 116 n1, '*noch einmal intensiv durchgearbeitet*'.

[32] *GAW*, pp. 517–18 (Shils, pp. 39–40).

explain their actual behaviour, he will have then to demonstrate empirically not only why those who don't act in accordance with those rules don't, but also why those who do, do. This will involve him, on Weber's view as on Collingwood's, in an account of the meaning which the observed behaviour has to those performing it; but this by itself will furnish only the preliminary part of the causal account which he will have to go on to give.

That even the history of art is, after all, explicable in principle by the common criteria of science is explicitly argued by Weber with reference to Gothic architecture. He cites the notion of 'the Gothic' as an example of an 'ideal type', which is 'ideal' not merely in the sense that no actual work of art exemplifies all of the characteristics implicit in the art-historian's term 'Gothic' but also in the sense that its meaning derives from the meaning which the art historian believes 'Gothic' architecture to have had for the artists who created and practised it. But from neither consideration does it follow that Gothic architecture or any other set of works of art is inexplicable. On the contrary: the conditions which principally determined the problems at which the Gothic artists set themselves to work were (in Weber's own words) 'the conjunction of this primarily technical revolution [the vault] with certain specific and largely socially and religiously conditioned feelings'.[33] It is true that the attempt to specify in full the necessary and sufficient conditions of any individual work of art would be futile. As Popper later put it, 'I don't wish to quarrel with the metaphysical determinist who would insist that every bar of Beethoven's work was determined by some combination of hereditary or environmental influences. Such an assertion is empirically insignificant, since no one could actually explain a single bar of his writing in this way' – a remark which echoes an almost identical dismissal by Weber of 'unthinking protestation of faith on behalf of metaphysical determinism' as irrelevant to the work of the practising historian.[34] But Weber is no more concerned than Popper to deny the unity of science on that account. The art historian is among other things concerned to identify under a common heading works of art which

[33] *GAW*, p. 507 (Shils, p. 30). The example recurs briefly in Weber's 'Introduction' to *The Protestant Ethic* (*GAR* I, 2–3 (Parsons, *PE*, p. 15)).
[34] Karl Popper, *The Open Society and Its Enemies* (3rd edn; London, 1957), II, 210; Weber's reference to *'unbedenklich formulierte protestatio fidei zugunsten des metaphysischen Determinismus'* is made in the critique of Knies (*GAW*, p. 137).

can be shown, within limits, to follow from identifiable initial conditions. Weber uses this particular example of architecture only for an illustration. But he did apply his own procedure in more detail in his studies in the history of music: in one of the reminiscences which we have of Weber at Heidelberg, Karl Loewenstein has described the occasion of his first visit to the Weber household in 1912 (wishing, as it happened, to see Marianne, and knowing nothing about her husband), when he was astonished to be treated by Max Weber to a thumbnail sociology of music, including the revelation that Bach's *Well-tempered Clavichord*, among other things, could be traced to identifiable 'rational and social foundations'.[35]

I shall have to return in more detail in the following section to Weber's doctrine of 'ideal types'. For the moment, I am concerned only to forestall any interpretation of his methodology which would leave him vulnerable to the charge that he did, after all, adhere to some version or other of 'intuitionism'; and to see still more clearly how, although he held that social-scientific explanation must have reference to the motives of those whose behaviour furnishes the explanandum, he repudiated intuitionism of whatever kind, it will be helpful to look briefly at the second of his two fundamental presuppositions – his individualism. This again is a topic which has aroused much controversy among more recent English-speaking philosophers, in this instance largely under the influence of Popper. But Weber already insisted, well before the self-styled 'methodological individualists', that although collective concepts may be usefully employed in the social sciences even though they cannot be precisely redefined in individual terms, propositions which employ collective concepts can be tested only by reference to individual behaviour. He accepted the now orthodox view that the reduction of sociological to psychological and even physiological laws is an empirical matter which only the course of future research can decide;[36] but he still held that the task of the sociologist is to

[35] Karl Loewenstein, *Max Weber's Political Ideas in the Perspective of Our Time* (Boston, 1966), p. 93.
[36] He had principally in mind the possibility that sociological explanation might turn out at some points to be reducible to biological. It is not that he was in any way receptive to 'social Darwinism': he repudiated it categorically in both his Inaugural Lecture in 1895 and his lecture on the decline of ancient civilisation in 1896, and the section of *Economy and Society* on the sociology of race is concerned to show racial attitudes to be a function of social or historical conditions. But both in the argument he had with the biologist Ploetz at the 1910 German Sociological Congress.

24

establish causal explanations of the social actions of individuals in terms of the meanings of those actions to the individuals themselves. Indeed, he at one point seems to imply that this is as much an advantage as a defect by comparison with the sciences of nature: the natural scientist is 'limited to the formulation of causal uniformities', whereas the social scientist has the good fortune to be studying a class of phenomena of which he is himself an instance, and about which he therefore knows something already.[37] To be sure, Weber is well aware of the risks of the 'imaginary experiment' and of the virtual impossibility of testing any interesting sociological hypothesis by means of an actual psychological experiment properly controlled.[38] He is also well aware of the limited and provisional character of imputations of cause and effect in complex historical sequences of social action. But the emphasis which he lays on 'understanding' derives not from a hankering after 'hermeneutics' in the style of Dilthey, but from a two-fold conviction that individuals, not collectivities, are the proper terms of sociological explanation and that where an action can be demonstrably assigned to an understandable sequence of motives this can already be regarded as furnishing some explanation of the behaviour observed.

This way of putting his position, however, raises one immediate philosophical difficulty which Weber never clearly resolves. If he regards correct attribution of motive to a designated individual as (within its context) an explanation of an action and he also regards explanation as causal, then he is presumably committed to the view that motives are causes. But he never says so in so many words. He doesn't explicitly advance the view of the traditional English empiricists that motives are identifiable mental events which consistently precede, and must therefore be held to be the causes of, identifiable items of behaviour – 'ghostly thrusts', as they were effectively to be caricatured by Ryle.[39] But nor does he advance the

---

(see *GASS*, pp. 456–62) and in his study of workers' output for the *Verein* he was careful to concede that biological determinants should not be ruled out altogether; and in the introductory section of *Economy and Society* he expressly remarks that if future research discloses hereditary 'racial' differences, however unlikely this may actually be, sociology will have to treat such facts as given, like physiological facts about nutrition or ageing: see *GAW*, p. 532 (Parsons, p. 94).

[37] *GAW*, pp. 540–1 (Parsons, pp. 103–4).
[38] *GAW*, p. 535 (Parsons, p. 97).
[39] Gilbert Ryle, *The Concept of Mind* (London, 1949).

opposite view that the connection between motives and actions is merely a logical one which therefore cannot (or so it is sometimes argued) be a relation of cause and effect at all. The likely answer is that he never considered the question in this way: after all, he could hardly have been expected to foresee the spate of discussion which it was to arouse among English-speaking philosophers of the 1950s and 1960s.[40] But since it is a question of obvious relevance to a critique of his methodology, I had better, even though I shall have to revert to it in the following section, say at once how I think Weber can be rescued from the imputation of inconsistency which it may be thought to raise.

There are two answers. The first is to follow those philosophers who suggest that the antithesis may not in fact be so stark as recent philosophical discussion has tended to make it. It is perfectly true that motives are not distinctive mental events of the kind that Hume or Mill may have thought they were. But it does not follow that there must then be the same sort of logical connection between 'He hated him' and 'He killed him' as there is between 'It was water-soluble and placed in water' and 'It dissolved'. The description of someone's behaviour which justifies the assertion that he has the motive (or as some philosophers might be prepared to say, 'consti-tutes' his having the motive) doesn't have to be identified with the description of what he does which, if he were not so motivated, he would not do.[41] The analogy with purposeful machines may be useful here. We do not, of course, wish to say of them that they have motives. But we do wish to say of them that their behaviour can be explained by reference to their prior state – which in this case is to say, their program. The program is self-evidently not an event; but why should it be held to follow that it does not therefore explain the machine's behaviour? Admittedly, it is not the whole story. Just as someone may be dissatisfied to be told that a man is waving his arm 'because' he is greeting a friend ('Yes, but what's

---

40 See H. L. A. Hart and A. M. Honoré, *Causation and the Law* (Oxford, 1959), Stuart Hampshire, *Thought and Action* (London, 1959), and A. I. Melden, *Free Action* (London, 1961), among others.

41 See Donald Davidson, 'Actions, Reasons and Causes', in May Brodbeck, ed., *Readings in the Philosophy of the Social Sciences* (New York, 1968), pp. 44–58, and A. J. Ayer, 'Man as a Subject for Science', in P. Laslett and W. G. Runciman, eds., *Philosophy, Politics and Society*, Third Series (Oxford, 1967), pp. 6–24.

causing him to greet his friend?'), so he may be dissatisfied to be told no more than that he is observing *machina speculatrix* homing in on the electric plug in order to recharge itself if what he wants to know is how and in accordance with what known or hypothesised scientific laws it has been programmed to do it. But the machine's behaviour isn't to be *identified* with the program; and no more is the man's behaviour with his motive. There is, therefore, nothing inconsistent in Weber's simultaneous belief that the attribution of motive is explanatory and that explanation requires a specification of causes.

These matters, however, are still controversial among philosophers, so that I ought perhaps not to assume quite so readily that the apparent inconsistency can be dissolved in this way. But the second answer is simply to say that even if it can't, Weber is not thereby convicted of seeking to replace causal analysis with empathetic intuition. Suppose that the connection between motives and actions is, after all, a logical one, as not only Idealist philosophers but also some Behaviourist psychologists still wish to maintain. The consequences for Weber's argument would be little more than verbal: what he calls (mistakenly, on this view) explanation in terms of motive should be called nothing more than the identification of the action (and its motive) which requires to be explained. We have already seen that Weber recognises the need for some such sort of identification just as unreservedly as Collingwood was to do; but we have also seen that, unlike Collingwood, he never conceives of the process of explanation as ending there. He could therefore afford to concede, if he had to, a change of terminology whereby the identification not merely of intention but of motive becomes a necessary preliminary to explanation but is refused the title of explanation itself. Let us take Weber's own example of a man chopping wood (which is, as it happens, conveniently similar to the sort of example later favoured by a number of English-speaking philosophers of action):[42] he may, says Weber, be working for a wage, getting in firewood for his own use, chopping for recreation or even working off a fit of temper. We decide between these alternatives without making reference to general laws. Yet it seems natural to say that in doing so we are to some degree, at any rate, explaining his behaviour: to say that he is working off a fit of

[42] *GAW*, p. 533 (Parsons, p. 95).

27

temper is to say why he is chopping wood. Similarly, if we know that a man is engaged in balancing a ledger we know why he is writing down arithmetical calculations (which of course we need also to 'understand' in a different sense which has nothing to do with causality). I myself doubt whether Weber felt any urge whatever to deny that these 'explanations' *are* causal.[43] But suppose for the sake of argument that he would have agreed, had the point been put to him, that he ought not to have spoken of motives in terms of what he calls 'causal adequacy at the level of meaning'. This would in no way require him – in fact, quite the contrary – to modify his view that empirically testable causal hypotheses are the stuff of the natural and the social sciences alike. He would need only to say that in the social sciences, unlike the natural, re-description in terms not merely of intention but of motive is (at least in the present state of our knowledge) indispensable to the correct identification of the explanandum and its assignation to the class of actions to which it belongs.

This discussion may seem rather remote from the sort of problem by which historians and sociologists are actually exercised. But to see how Weber's procedure can be directly applied to a central topic in the social sciences it is enough to cite the one to which, in the next section of *Economy and Society*, he himself applies it. From the concept of social action Weber derives the concept of a social relationship, which in a well-known definition he takes to consist in the meaningful behaviour of a plurality of persons all of whom take account of each other's behaviour in their own, so that when we speak of some particular institutional form of social relationship, whether a marriage or a state, we are speaking of the probability of action appropriate to the meaning which the social relationship has to those involved in it. In the case of a state, these actions have meaning in terms of a belief in the existence of a legitimate order which claims binding authority over all action taking place within the area of its jurisdiction. A state, therefore, is (in what is perhaps the most famous of all Weber's definitions) a compulsory association which successfully claims a monopoly of the legitimate use of force within a given territory. This definition,

---

[43] In fact Weber would, I suspect, have agreed with the suggestion that the citation of motives is explanatory in a causal sense whereas the citation of intentions is 'explanatory in a non-causal sense': see Quentin Skinner, 'On Performing and Explaining Linguistic Actions', *Philosophical Quarterly* XXI (1971), 20–1.

derived as it is from the initial conception of social action, preserves both the individualism and the subjectivism of its more primitive components,[44] and it leads in turn to Weber's threefold distinction between the traditional, charismatic and rational-legal types of legitimate *Herrschaft*,[45] whose occurrence in different combinations and to different degrees calls to be historically, and therefore causally, explained.

Now it may be said that this threefold distinction, however widely praised, has not led to the establishment of any laws of behaviour which would establish it as definitive. But this is hardly a relevant objection to the presuppositions from which it is derived, since Weber did not believe that it, or any alternative to it, would ever be capable of producing laws of such a kind. It may be that (as I shall later argue) his reasons for this view were in part misplaced since it is on presumptive psychological, rather than sociological, laws that historical explanation depends; but his mistake was not that of failing to discern some alternative, and more 'objective', typology of domination by means of which general laws about régimes as such could after all have been formulated. The virtue of the concept of charismatic domination, in particular, is simply that it identifies one basis of legitimacy which, depending on the particular historical circumstances in which it arises, will make only a certain range of subsequent political changes likely or even possible. For the reasons which I gave in the introductory section I don't propose to pursue the substantive issue further here. But however much Weber's ideas about 'charismatic domination' may stand in need of supersession

---

[44] Cf. *GAW*, p. 200 (Shils, p. 99): 'When we ask what corresponds to the idea of the "State" in empirical reality, we find an infinity of diffuse and discrete human actions and passions, partly unique and partly recurrent relationships which are both factually and legally regulated, all held together by an idea – the belief in norms and relations of authority of men over men which are or ought to be binding.'

[45] The discussion of domination in the opening sections of *Economy and Society* is in fact only a preliminary to a later and more extensive treatment of it, and the classification which Weber applies initially is that of his fourfold typology of action rather than the subsequent classification in terms of traditional, charismatic, and rational-legal. It may be that a satisfactory reconciliation is possible, but for the purposes of this essay it makes no difference whether or not it is. There is also a difference of opinion among Weber's commentators over the translation of *Herrschaft*: Parsons, despite some misgivings (see his p. 131 n59), renders it as 'authority', but Aron (*op. cit.* II, 235–6) prefers 'domination', I think rightly.

or amendment (as he would have been the first to accept),[46] his typology can be used to generate testable empirical propositions about the causes and consequences of particular systems of legitimacy. To this degree, at least, his own substantive sociology must be admitted to vindicate his emphasis on individual motives as the proper basis of concept-formation in the sciences of human behaviour.

The contrast with the sociological method of Durkheim and his successors should by now be too obvious to call for extended comment. Durkheim did, it is true, share Weber's subjectivism to the extent that he too, in his fashion, sought to explain human institutions in terms of the sentiments which they implant and sustain in the people who constitute them. But the difference, of course, lies in Durkheim's holism. By Weber's standards, Durkheim's sociology is fatally vitiated by its illegitimate reification of collective concepts; by Durkheim's standards, Weber's sociology is fatally vitiated by its misplaced reductionism. That Weber's presumptions are sound and Durkheim's mistaken follows to the degree that 'methodological individualism' is now generally conceded to be almost trivially true. But it would be wrong to dismiss Durkeim's arguments as entirely without foundation, and the contrast may still be instructive if so drawn as to show just how much of Durkheim's general argument can, and how much cannot, be retained without incompatibility with Weber's.

CRAP.

The classical holist position, as set out by Durkheim in his preface to the second edition of the *Rules of Sociological Method*, rests on the claim that the properties of aggregates are 'freely admitted in the other realms of nature' to 'reside not in the original elements but in the totality formed by their union'.[47] The properties of the living cell are not properties of its constituents; the properties of water are not properties of hydrogen and oxygen; and in the same way, the properties of society are not properties of the individuals who compose it. Now all this is perfectly true. But what Durkheim failed to see was not merely that he was asserting

[46] In the lecture on 'Science as a Vocation' he remarks that everyone engaged in academic work knows that his work will be outdated in ten, twenty or fifty years at the outside: see *GAW*, p. 576 (G & M, p. 138), and a similar disclaimer in the 'Introduction' to the *Protestant Ethic* (*GAR* I, 13–14 (Parsons, *PE*, p. 28)).

[47] Emile Durkheim, *The Rules of Sociological Method* (ed. Catlin; Chicago, 1938), p. xviii.

something which nobody (least of all Weber) would wish to deny, but that it doesn't undermine the arguments for reductionism. Nobody denies that the properties of chemical compounds are not the properties of their physical constituents; but the fact is that, as we now know, chemistry *is* reducible to physics. In the same way, nobody denies that the properties of groups, organisations and institutions, whether statistical or structural, are not the properties of the individuals who compose them: individual persons don't have birth-rates or median per capita incomes or sociometric patterns any more than they have democratic constitutions or priestly castes or procedures of collective bargaining. But from this obvious truth of logic, it follows neither that sociology is irreducible to psychology nor that thought and action can be predicated of anything other than individual self-conscious beings. Weber is as insistent as Durkheim that sociology and psychology are separate levels of analysis, and that even if reduction does turn out to be possible sociologists will not have lost their *raison d'être* (any more, we might say, than chemists have lost theirs because we can now reduce chemistry to physics). Important though the differences between Durkheim and Weber are, there is no need to exaggerate them, as so often happens in social theory, to the point where one of them is required to deny a perfectly obvious truth asserted by the other. The moral to be drawn from the contrast between them, as from the contrast between Weber and Collingwood, is rather that Weber's method avoids one serious and even fatal mistake which Durkheim's doesn't. Durkheim's claims for the autonomy of sociology can be sustained only at the cost of his claims for its empirical standing. Weber, by contrast, whatever his other mistakes may have been, is able to ensure that no proposition can be formulated in accordance with his method which is not in principle amenable to empirical test by virtue of its reference to the observable behaviour of individual persons. *Even if all tests lead to rejections of Weber's proposit-*

From this preliminary outline, it should be clear both that *ions !* Weber's subjectivism did not involve any claim that the validation of historical or social-scientific discovery rests on empathetic intuition and that his concomitant rejection of psychologism did not expose him to the same charge of philosophising (in the pejorative sense) on which Durkheim's critics have rightly convicted him. But it still remains for me to show how he came to hold that there *is* a difference of kind between the natural and social sciences even

31

though the latter must proceed by the formulation and public test of empirical causal hypotheses about the behaviour of designated individuals; and to do this, it is necessary to look in closer detail at the three interrelated concepts in terms of which the central tenets of his methodology are formulated: 'ideal type', 'understanding' and 'value-relevance'.

III

Weber's notion of ideal types has from the beginning attracted more discussion and controversy both inside and outside Germany even than the other two of the three.[48] Almost all of his commentators have accused him of one or another of several different confusions. But they have too often failed to consider whether the distinctions which they hold that he ought to have made are in fact the most important for his purposes. It is perfectly true that his ideal types operate at widely different levels of generality;[49] that they cover systems of belief as well as systems of action;[50] and that it is not always clear from Weber's discussion when they are to be construed as concepts and when as statements.[51] But these questions are only incidental to Weber's own principal argument, which is that the construction of ideal types, whatever their various forms, is not merely indispensable to the social sciences, but also, and more surprisingly, peculiar to them. Now the second of these claims, so stated, is palpably incorrect, since idealisations, both in the sense of notional entities supposed to instantiate extreme values of one or more variables and in the sense of propositions about how such entities would (if they existed) behave are common in the physical sciences. But to leave the matter there would be to miss Weber's point. If we modify it by saying only that he believes the construction of ideal types to stand in a different relation to theory-construction in social-scientific and in natural-scientific explanation, then

[48] Contrast, for example, two of his earliest English-speaking commentators: to Lowell L. Bennion, *Max Weber's Methodology* (Paris, 1933), p. 168, Weber's ideal types 'lack systematization. They are indefinite in number and offer us no differentiation in regard to their importance to one another'; but to Howard Becker, 'Culture Case Study and Ideal-Typical Method: with special reference to Max Weber', *Social Forces* XII (1934), 405, 'it may be said with confidence that this method has stood every test that can legitimately be applied to it'.

[49] Aron, *op. cit.* II, 202–4.

[50] Talcott Parsons, *The Structure of Social Action* (New York, 1937), pp. 604ff, following A. von Schelting, *Max Webers Wissenschaftslehre* (Tübingen, 1934).

[51] Richard S. Rudner, *Philosophy of Social Science* (Englewood Cliffs, N.J., 1966), p. 54 n1.

we need not take him to be denying that the well-tested theories of the developed physical sciences make use of idealisations also, even if he really believed this in 1903.

As Weber applies them in practice, ideal types are both terms and statements, and just as in the natural sciences the one shades over into the other. The notion of an ideal gas, to take the most familiar example, is accorded meaning within the kinetic theory of gases because Boyle's law, which is derivable from the kinetic theory, furnishes adequate grounds for asserting what would be the behaviour of an ideal gas if there were to be such a thing (which there isn't). Or to take an example from the biological sciences, comparative anatomists and ethologists can legitimately postulate the ideal type of a species by reference to the anatomical and behavioural structure which would instantiate all of the features known to have survival value in terms of the theory of natural selection, even if no such member of the species in question has ever been found. In the same way, the meaning given to social-scientific idealisations rests on a presumption that if there were such things as pure cases (which there aren't) we could say how they would function – which means, to Weber, how individual members of societies with designated attributes would behave under what he calls 'Utopian' conditions. There is not the same backing for such assertions in social as in natural science; but this is to say no more than that natural, and particularly physical, science has much better theories. It makes no difference that the ideal types with which social scientists characteristically operate are so much more tentative and so much less precise. Nor does it make any difference that they can be of such various forms. The idealisation may consist in supporting that only one motive is operative among the members of the hypothetical system, as in the case of the ideal type of 'charismatic domination', or that all of a designated set of characteristics can be predicated of the hypothetical system, as in the case of a 'pure' bureaucracy. Equally, the idealisation may be at so very general a level as 'rational' behaviour or at so very particular a level as 'capitalism', which may have been instantiated only once in a form even approaching the extreme values of the set of variables which would constitute the ideal case. But if the test of an ideal type is whether or not it can be used to formulate validated causal explanations of the actual course of observed events, these differences are not matters of principle but merely of detail.

34

Accordingly, to see where, in Weber's view, the distinctiveness of social-scientific idealisation resides, it is necessary to see how he links it to his other two central methodological concepts – understanding and value-relevance – and how these are connected in turn with his initial recognition that the subject-matter of the social sciences is at once subjective and open-ended. He is at pains to point out not only that there is no such thing as a theory of human action of the form of the theories of chemistry or physics, but also that the explanation of human action, unlike the explanation of gases, will constantly require the formulation of new terms. There could never be a social science in whose terms we could formulate the future concepts of social science itself, and it is futile to look for a closed system of sociological concepts on some misconceived analogy with a science like classical mechanics:[52] social science must proceed by 'a perpetual process of reconstruction of those concepts in terms of which we seek to lay hold of reality'.[53] Accordingly, the distinguishing feature of ideal type construction in the social sciences is that it requires conceptual innovation derived from an 'ideal' extrapolation from what Weber sometimes refers to as the 'flux' of human, and therefore cultural, history.

Now the connection between the impossibility of quasi-mechanistic Laplacean laws of human history and the necessity for sociological, and therefore cultural, concepts with singular referents of the type of 'the Reformation' or 'Ancient Greece' is clear enough. But the trouble arises when Weber goes on to suggest that because cultural evolution is subjective and open-ended the social scientist not only need not but cannot rest his explanations on general laws, and cannot frame his explanations without implicit dependence upon presuppositions of a 'value-relevant' kind. The first hint of danger lies in the contrast which he draws between the hypotheses of natural science and the ideal-typical models of social science in terms of the directly testable character of the first and the unfalsifiability of the second. I have already remarked that it is true that historians, in contrast to natural scientists, are untroubled by the fact that their explanations can seldom be generalised: a historical event is no less explicable in their eyes if it is exceptional, or

---

[52] Mechanics is explicitly cited by Weber as a paradigm for the exact sciences at the very beginning of the essay on Roscher (*GAW*, p. 4); cf. *GAW*, p. 262 (Shils, p. 160).
[53] *GAW*, p. 207 (Shils, p. 105).

even unique, whereas an exception to the law-like generalisations of science is altogether more disturbing. Such an exception may, of course, signal a need for a radical revision of accepted theory; but it is more likely to goad the community of scientists to a determined attempt to find an *ad hoc* hypothesis which would enable the existing theory to be saved. In this sense, Weber is right both when he points out that a hypothetical natural law which misfires in a single definitive instance is undermined once and for all[54] and when he describes historians' explanations in terms of the 'imputation' of causes rather than deduction from known causal laws. But when he goes on to say that the ideal-typical model of a competitive economy is immune to falsification because it isn't about anything real,[55] and when he claims that the ultimate aim of concept-formation in the social sciences is knowledge of the 'cultural significance' of concrete historical events,[56] he runs the risk of undermining his simultaneous commitment to the universality of cause and effect. Weber's remarks in the editorial of 1904 have to be read in the context of the long-standing German debate about economics between Schmoller on behalf of the 'Historical' and Menger on behalf of the 'Classical' school; but whatever his reasons for coming down to this degree on the side of Schmoller, Weber's argument has to be corrected as it stands. Debate has, in fact, continued among economists about the propriety of constructing models whose assumptions are deliberately unreal. But, as we have seen, the test of an ideal type must be the part which it does or could play in a fully developed and well-tested theory, and it is on these grounds that it should be amended or discarded by the practising social scientist. If the assumptions built into the ideal type aren't realistic, he needs to have some good reasons for saying that they might as well be: a hypothesis which assumes, say, a degree of 'rationality' on the part of buyers and sellers which is known not in fact to obtain will not be successful for long if it holds only by coincidence. Weber is misleading on this point not so much because he fails to spell out the distinctions between different kinds of social-scientific idealisations as because he fails to spell out the relation between his 'ideal types' and the underlying regularities which must somewhere be

[54] *GAW*, p. 131.
[55] *Ibid.*
[56] *GAW*, p. 214 (Shils, p. 111); and cf. the incidental remarks on the use of the concept of 'cultural levels' in the paper on the social structure of ancient Germany (*GASW*, p. 517).

presupposed if his own assumption of causal explicability is to be sustained.

If, therefore, we correct his discussion by denying that ideal types are peculiar to the social sciences we remain free to agree with him that the idealisations of the social sciences differ in some important respect from those of the natural. But his own account of this difference still needs to be further corrected, since it rests on a persistent confusion between value-judgements and theoretical pre- ^{NB} suppositions. Indeed, this confusion seems to have been responsible in part for his conviction that the problems of idealisation are unique to the sciences of man. As is well known, he insisted cate- gorically on the logical independence of judgements of fact and judgements of value and the consequent irrelevance of the social scientist's own aesthetic or moral opinions to the validity of his proffered explanations of human conduct. Yet the social scientist's values do still, according to Weber, enter into his investigation at a prior stage, since the scope and form of his investigation must depend upon 'value-relevant' presuppositions neither derivable from nor testable against the empirical findings which issue from it. To the obvious question 'why *value*-relevant?', Weber's answer is that since the social sciences are concerned with events, objects or states of a kind to which the possibility of evaluation inherently attaches, the social scientist can only formulate his investigation by reference to what has value to himself as a 'cultural' being. But what exactly does this mean? In what sense is the term 'value' being used?

Of all the topics covered in Weber's writings on methodology, this is unfortunately the one on which he lays himself most open to misinterpretation. In the essay on 'The Meaning of "Value- freedom"' he says distinctly that he does not mean that values enter into scientific enquiry either in the sense that science aspires to logically and empirically correct and therefore 'valuable' results[57] or in the sense that the selection of a topic for study already

---

[57] It is, perhaps, debatable whether it is 'obvious that "valid" is an evalu- ative expression', as more recently argued by J. O. Urmson, 'Some Questions Concerning Validity', in Antony Flew, ed., *Essays in Con- ceptual Analysis* (London, 1956), p. 127. But Weber seems to have held first, that this is indeed obvious (cf. *GASS*, p. 449); second, that it is not on this question that the social sciences differ in kind from the natural; and third, that this 'value' is no less arbitrary than any other. On this third point, he seems as so often to be following Simmel.

involves a value-judgement.[58] But despite his indignation at being so read, he does say things which make the interpretation excusable. In the editorial of 1904 he had spoken of the pursuit of social-scientific knowledge as resting on the presupposition of the value of scientific truth as such;[59] and in the 'Value-freedom' essay itself he speaks of 'value-relevance' as referring to the 'philosophical interpretation of the specific academic interest which determines the *selection* [my italics] and formulation of an empirical investigation'.[60] The answer to these apparent contradictions, however, must be that to Weber neither issue is one which distinguishes the social sciences from the natural. It is quite true both that the selection of a topic for investigation is a matter of subjective preference and that the practice of science presupposes such norms as 'correct' procedure, 'legitimate' inference, 'valid' reasoning and so forth. But Weber is concerned with a difference at the level of 'presuppositions' where he holds that the social scientist's formulation of his hypotheses about his chosen topic cannot but have relevance to his 'values' in a way that the natural scientist's does not have to his.

Now it is true, and indeed obvious, that the things about which social scientists try to construct theories are things about which we all do make value-judgements; so that in one sense values can certainly be said to be more 'relevant' to social than to natural science. But it does not follow from this that the concepts and hypotheses of the social, unlike the natural, scientist must actually derive from his values. Weber himself seems so ready to accept the plausibility of the transition that he never spells it out in full. But it appears to rest on an implicit sequence which might be summarised something like this: the social sciences are historical sciences of culture; social scientists do not, and cannot, have a theory of culture in the sense that chemists have theories of chemistry or physicists of physics; they must, however, have presuppositions which dictate the terms of their proposed hypotheses; since these cannot be drawn from a theory which doesn't exist they must be drawn from somewhere else; accordingly, their source can only lie in the criteria of 'cultural significance' (*Kulturbedeutung*), and therefore the 'cultural value-ideas' (*Kulturwertideen*) which

[58] *GAW*, p. 485 (Shils, pp. 10–11).
[59] *GAW*, p. 213 (Shils, pp. 110–11); cf. *GAW*, p. 583 (G & M, p. 143).
[60] *GAW*, p. 497 (Shils, p. 22).

every social scientist brings to the subject-matter he has chosen to study.[61]

It may well be that Weber would not have accepted this as a fair summary of his position. But it is as plausible a formulation as I think can be made, and it is still mistaken. If explicability in principle has once been accepted, it doesn't matter where the social scientist's concepts and therefore his hypotheses come from but only whether the hypotheses are so framed that in principle, at least, they are capable of empirical disconfirmation.[62] Even if it is true that social-scientific explanation is, in Windelband's term, 'idiographic' it is not therefore 'value-relevant' in Weber's sense. Idiographic explanation is commonplace in the natural sciences, too: classical mechanics is no more a model for the geologist than for the art historian.[63] Weber is not saying anything which would nowadays be regarded as controversial when he says that 'every historical comparison assumes that a choice has been made by reference to 'cultural significance' which, by excluding an infinite number of given facts, both general and particular, determines the purpose and direction of the imputation of causes'[64] any more than when he says that 'imputation of causes' obviously does not proceed by way of 'simple observation of the course of events, if

[61] At *GAW*, p. 175 (Shils, p. 76), Weber actually says that 'The concept of culture is a value-concept'. He also explicitly repudiates as a 'remarkable misunderstanding' of Rickert the view expressed by a writer in Ostwald's *Annalen der Naturphilosophie* that 'value-relevance' is nothing more than subsumption under general categories such as 'state', 'religion' or 'art' (*GAW*, p. 252 (Shils, p. 150)). In this, of course, he is quite right: he *did* mean more than this, and the criticism is well taken only in the sense that for the logic of sociological explanation he had no need to.

[62] The precise point at which Weber went wrong can perhaps be more clearly highlighted by contrasting Wittgenstein's remark in the *Philosophical Investigations* (Oxford, 1958), para. 570 that 'Concepts lead us to make investigations; are the expression of our interest, and direct our interest' with Gunnar Myrdal's remark in his *Value in Social Theory* (London, 1958), p. 1 that 'There is no way of studying social reality other than from the viewpoint of human ideas. . . The value connotation of our main concepts represents our interest in a matter, gives direction to our thought and significance to our inferences.' Weber would have agreed with both. But whereas the first implies nothing at variance with scientific method, the second is rendered gratuitously misleading by the insertion of the term 'value'.

[63] Cf. C. F. A. Pantin, *The Relations Between the Sciences* (Cambridge, 1968), ch. I.

[64] *GAW*, p. 232 (Shils, p. 130).

39

one understands by this a "presuppositionless" mental "photo-graph" of all the physical and psychological events in the relevant part of time and space'.[65] Nobody any longer believes in the *tabula rasa* of old-fashioned empiricism, and Weber himself is well aware that a 'complete' account of the phenomenon under study is equally out of the question in natural science.[66] Both natural and social science involve selective abstraction; both rest on theoretical pre-suppositions not derivable from the observations which they are invoked in order to explain; both are concerned to explain unique configurations of events as well as lawlike regularities; both involve an initial selection of the particular problems to be studied which, for what little it matters, is arbitrary by definition. Moreover – a point which I think was somewhere in Weber's mind, although he never stated it in quite this way – both involve the application of what Nagel calls 'characterising' as distinct from 'appraising' value-judgements;[67] that is, both may require arbitrary decisions as to whether some putatively standardised condition is or is not exemplified by the case in question, as when, in Nagel's example, a biologist hesitates over the application of the term 'anaemic'. Weber's confusion between theoretical presuppositions and 'appraising' value-judgements arises because having once pointed out the undeniable differences between the social (and therefore historical and cultural) sciences and an implicit, and rather restricted, model of natural science, he concludes from them that the theoretical presuppositions of the social scientist must derive from his 'cultural value-ideas' about 'cultural significance'. But the answer is simply that the social scientist's *Kulturwertideen* are no more relevant to the scientific validity of his reported findings than the *Kulterwertideen* of the natural scientist to his.

A plausible-looking example for Weber's case might be, say, the Marxist use of the term 'class': Marxist social theory, although its claims are explicitly rested on empirical evidence, still treats 'class conflict' as an axiomatic characteristic of liberal-democratic or 'bourgeois' society, and it can hardly be denied that 'class', in obvious contrast to a physical concept like 'mass', is often laden with evaluative overtones. But however many adherents of Marxist social theory may, as a recognised matter of fact, be drawn to it

[65] *GAW*, p. 273 (Shils, p. 171).
[66] *GAW*, pp. 66–7.
[67] Nagel, *op. cit.* p. 492.

40

because of their moral views about the relation between the owners of capital and the vendors of labour, it still does not follow that a theory in which the term 'class' features is derived from 'evaluative' presuppositions in the way that Weber seeks to maintain. As Weber would be the first to agree, the non-Marxist is logically free to agree that class conflict is intrinsic to bourgeois society while holding this to be a thoroughly good thing. Why, therefore, is the acceptance of 'class' as a theoretical term a matter of its 'relevance to values'? It may admittedly be used in the would-be theory in a proposition which is made true by definition. But if so, this is no different by the standards of science from, say, a decision to take Newton's First Law of Motion as definitionally true. The detailed articulation of any scientific theory requires selection of the set of terms which is to be logically primitive within it. The test (which, for other reasons, Newtonian theory passes rather better than Marxist) is the same: do the hypotheses generated by the relevant set of connected propositions stand up to attempted empirical refutation? It is possible, and even likely, that evidence which could be generally agreed to furnish a decisive test of the hypotheses alleged to be derivable from the theory is rather harder to find in the social-scientific case, with the result that those whose hopes are pinned to one suggested explanation rather than another because of their ideological predilections will have not only a stronger motive but a better opportunity to keep their candidate in the field. But this, again, is 'relevance to values' in quite another sense from Weber's. His confusion of theoretical presuppositions with value-judgements leaves him with an irreconcilable dilemma. Either values are peculiarly relevant to the social sciences, but in a sense which makes no difference to the standing of the theory in question, or they are by definition built in to all theories, natural-scientific and social-scientific alike. In neither case can the distinguishing feature of social-scientific theories or, in the absence of theories, idiographic explanations be claimed to reside in their 'relevance' to the 'values' of the social scientist who propounds them.

There is, however, still the second and related consideration which Weber advances and which I have so far left to one side. Despite his rejection of intuitionism, Weber does still regard 'understanding' as peculiar to social as against natural science, and he sees this as involving the social scientist's *Kulturwertideen* even

41

though, once again, this has nothing to do with any intrusion of his personal preferences into his empirically testable claims. Weber therefore insists that although the art historian's views as to whether a work of art is good or bad have nothing to do with the validity of his scientific judgements, he must still have the *capacity* to form an appraisive value-judgement about them.[68] Is it not plausible, therefore, to claim that the social scientist's theoretical presuppositions must be 'value-relevant' at least to the degree that his theoretical terms are necessarily 'subjective'?

The answer to this slightly different question is again negative. But to see why, it is necessary to go further than I did in the previous section into what Weber means by 'understanding'; and for this purpose, it will be as well to revert to the examples which he uses himself in the discussion of social action in *Economy and Society*. I have stressed already that a characteristic explanation of human action as Weber conceives of it will refer an action performed in some social or institutional context to the motive of the agent performing it, as when we explain a man's chopping wood by showing that he is collecting it for fuel or a man's adding columns of figures by showing that he is trying to balance a ledger. Further, I have suggested that Weber regarded such explanations as (already) properly causal ones, even though his position on the relation of motives to actions is not entirely clear. But there are two related distinctions which he draws over and above the distinction between those explanations which do and those which don't have reference to general laws. The first of these is between 'direct' (*aktuell*) and 'explanatory' (*erklärend*) understanding: understanding the actions of the wood-chopper or the ledger clerk is 'explanatory' understanding, while understanding the proposition 'twice two is four', or a facial expression or gesture signifying anger, or a man's reaching for a door knob or aiming a gun is 'direct' understanding. Now this is an odd set of examples, since it juxtaposes the understanding of an arithmetical proposition or an expression of emotion with the understanding of human actions to which, it might seem more natural to suppose, 'explanatory' understanding is the appropriate one of the pair. But it is, I think, clear from Weber's discussion as a whole what he is after. We have already seen that it is in part, at least, a verbal issue at what point the identification of an action slides over into its explanation: to say 'he is shutting the door' is,

[68] *GAW*, p. 510 (Shils, p. 33); cf. *GAW*, p. 250 n1 (Shils, p. 148 n23).

42

as I read Weber, to account for his turning of the knob by *identifying* the (intentional) action which then requires to be explained *as an action*, just as in the example of the priest celebrating mass to say 'he is celebrating mass' is to account for his (intentional) words and gestures but not to explain either what has motivated him to celebrate mass or how it comes about that such a thing goes on in the culture in question in the first place. For Weber, sociological explanation begins when the observer attributes a motive to the agent, and ends when an empirical demonstration is afforded both that this *was* the motive and how (in terms of the particular hypotheses which the sociologist selects out of the limitless range of possible causes and effects) it came to be so. 'Direct' understanding, therefore, is a preliminary to the attribution of motive; and the attribution of motive involves, to Weber, answering the question 'why is he multiplying two and two?', 'why is he grimacing in anger?', 'why is he shutting the door?' or 'why is he aiming the gun?', as opposed to 'what is he doing in making the marks "$2 \times 2 = 4$" on the paper?', 'what is he doing in contracting his eyebrows?,'[69] 'what is he doing in putting his hand on that knob?' or 'what is he doing in lifting up the gun and pointing it in that direction?'. It is, of course, possible to answer the latter set of questions wrongly just as readily as the former. But the distinction which Weber seems to wish to draw is that between identifying an action by reference to its meaning, and thus its intention, and explaining it by reference to its motive in some at least prospectively causal sense.

The second distinction, however, is also a little puzzling at first sight. Weber begins by offering an explicit but rather unsatisfying definition of a motive as a 'complex of subjective meaning' (*Sinnzusammenhang*: I have followed Parsons's translation) which 'appears to the agent himself or the observer to be a meaningful ground (*sinnhaft* "Grund") of the behaviour'.[70] He then draws the distinction between 'adequate in terms of meaning' (*sinnhaft adequät*) and 'adequate in terms of cause' (*kausal adequät*), and gives as an example a correct solution to an arithmetical problem

---

[69] Cf. Ryle, *op. cit.* p. 74: ' "He frowned intentionally" does not report the occurrence of two episodes. It reports the occurrence of one episode, but one of a very different character from that reported by "he frowned involuntarily", though the frowns might be as photographically similar as you please.'

[70] *GAW*, p. 536 (Parsons, p. 98).

whose correctness is a matter of the first and whose probability of in fact being the solution arrived at is a matter of the second. It is again fairly clear what Weber is after: I have already cited from his critique of Stammler his discussion of 'following a rule', where he emphasises the distinction between the normative content of a rule and the regularity of behaviour in accordance with it. But how does it relate to the distinction between 'direct' and 'explanatory' understanding? In the critique of Stammler, Weber also insists that from the standpoint of causal explanation it makes no difference whether institutional regularities of behaviour are the result of self-conscious compliance with a rule or not;[71] and this assertion may, at first sight, seem incompatible with his emphasis on 'understanding'. But although Weber's discussion at this point is again not as clear as one might wish, it is not necessarily inconsistent. The connecting link is provided by the concept of *Sinnzusammenhang*: 'adequacy in terms of meaning' furnishes 'explanatory understanding' where the *Sinnzusammenhang* attributed to the agent is recognised by the observer, who can therefore deduce from it the consequences which will follow *if* the agent acts consistently in terms of it.[72] This, however, is something which like any hypothesis based on 'explanatory understanding' has to be tested against the evidence before it can be claimed to be vindicated even provisionally in terms of 'causal adequacy'. It is, therefore, one possible explanation of the agent's behaviour among many; and although it is one of a kind with which sociologists or historians are particularly concerned, it by no means rules out the possibility of an equally well-founded causal explanation which has no reference whatever to 'adequacy in terms of meaning'. If the agent's *Sinnzusammenhang* is 'rational' in the observer's terms – as in the example of an arithmetical calculation or of a pursuit of some technical end by the means known to be most efficacious for it – then so much the better. But not only does a hypothesis derived from this have to be tested like any other;

---

[71] *GAW*, pp. 323–8.

[72] It is a pity that in *Economy and Society* Weber doesn't revert to the detailed discussion of 'rules of a game' in the critique of Stammler. In the sort of example which he uses there, and which anticipates much similar discussion by Wittgenstein and others, we might say that the explanation of a chess-player's having two pawns in a row is *sinnhaft adequät* if it refers to the rules for taking an opponent's piece but not *kausal adequät* if we don't know, say, that it was knocked there unnoticed and by mistake. See also *GAW*, pp. 443–4.

there is in any case no reason to assume that 'rational' motives predominate in human conduct.[73]

This view of sociological explanation can be well illustrated from Weber's analysis of the *Verein's* study of industrial workers, which as far as it goes is perfectly consistent with his precepts. The behaviour to be explained in this instance is workers' output. Weber distinguishes between explanation in terms of the 'rational' purposes of workers who deliberately adjust their output in accordance with these purposes, changes in the environment which may be susceptible to experimental manipulation and exercise a 'psychophysical' influence on output, and unconscious motives which are nevertheless psychologically 'understandable' and may need to be taken into account just as much as those which are overtly 'rational'. His discussion betrays a certain hesitancy about just what a successful explanation of variations in output would look like if it could be found (and the *Verein's* enquiry had certainly failed to find it). But such open-minded hesitancy is only too appropriate in view of the state of social-scientific knowledge not merely in Weber's time but to this day. Not only was he careful to concede that biological explanation might turn out either to underlie some ostensible sociological differences or to account for some residual part of the variation in some categories of behaviour, but he willingly acknowledged the potential importance of the work of both Kraepelin and Freud, despite his substantial reservations about the latter.[74] He still wishes to maintain that hypotheses in terms of self-conscious motives and purposes and the social conditions which generate them are those with which the social scientist is concerned, and that they involve the 'understanding' of the behaviour in question in a way that the hypotheses of natural science do not. But this means neither that they are purely arbitrary nor that they exclude or are irreconcilable with the explanations of behaviour which psychologists, physiologists or biologists may succeed in vindicating in their own terms. It may be that, as I have suggested already,

[73] *GAW*, p. 544 (Parsons, p. 107).
[74] See *GASS*, p. 249; and cf. the letter to Edgar Jaffé of 13 September 1907 reproduced by Baumgarten, *op. cit.* pp. 644–8 in which Weber expresses the view that Freud's ideas could be, but aren't yet, of major significance for 'a whole series' of topics in cultural, and particularly religious, history. He himself makes use at least once of an unmistakably Freudian idea when he says that the Gnostic mysteries 'clearly appear to have been a sublimated masturbatory substitute for the orgies of the peasantry' (*W & G* I, 307 (Fischoff, p. 124)).

Weber was too ready to reject the possible dependence of sociological on psychological explanation. Not only did he have a rather restricted definition of psychology, but he thought of psychology as merely one among the many different sciences in addition to history or sociology themselves from whose point of view a specific sequence of human behaviour can also be studied. In the example which he uses in the critique of Meyer, Caesar's death can be explained from the standpoint of physiology as well as of history; and at a certain level it must be, since it is a physiological, not a sociological, truth that a stabbing such as Caesar suffered is bound to be fatal.[75] But as Weber himself describes it, the sociologist's *verstehende* explanation of what interests *him* about such an event is still an empirical causal explanation just as much as the others, even though it is couched in terms of 'subjective' motives, norms and rules. It is not, therefore, whatever Weber may say, a matter of 'value-relevance' any more than is the lack of reference to general laws.

However mistaken, on the other hand, Weber may have been about the connection between his notions of 'understanding' and 'value-relevance', it is still as little to the point when his Positivist critics accuse him of requiring the social scientist to re-experience the motives which he has identified after the manner of Dilthey[76] as when his Idealist critics accuse him of failing to develop a 'constitutive phenomonology of the natural attitude' after the manner of Husserl.[77] In the course of his methodological writings, Weber three times repeats the dictum of Simmel that 'one need not be Caesar in order to understand him'. It is true that the word 'understand' has a number of different senses, and is sometimes so used that it is by definition impossible for someone to 'understand', say, the joy of requited love or the humiliation of defeat in battle if these things have never in fact happened to him. But this sense of the word is precisely the one which Weber does *not* mean when he says that understanding is indispensable to sociological explanation. What he *does* mean is that to explain the ledger clerk balanc-

---

[75] *GAW*, p. 272 (Shils, p. 170).

[76] E.g. Nagel (*op. cit.* pp. 480–5).

[77] The phrase is taken from the criticism of Weber by Alfred Schutz, *Collected Papers*, I: *The Problem of Social Reality* (ed. Natanson; The Hague, 1962), p. 138, citing Husserl's 'Nachwort zu meinen *Ideen*', *Jahrbuch für Philosophie und Phenomenologische Forschung* XI (1930), 567.

ing his ledger you must understand the meaning and application at once of the terms 'balance' and 'ledger' and of the terms designating the possible motives by which the balancing of ledgers may be inspired. This understanding involves, in his view, something more than is involved in coming to understand the meaning and use of the theoretical terms of a natural science; but it doesn't actually require an apprenticeship served in a counting-house, useful for the purpose though that might happen to be.

This still leaves it to be settled just what the difference consists in. But for my immediate purpose, the point is that Weber is wrong not because he claims that the understanding of such terms involves something over and above what is involved in the understanding of the terms of natural science, but because he claims that it involves 'relevance to values'. His most forthright statements of this are in the editorial of 1904, and as we have seen he did slightly modify his position thereafter. But in the opening sections of *Economy and Society* he still unequivocally insists that one must know at the outset of a 'functional' account of some particular feature of a culture 'what a "king", "official", "entrepreneur", "procurer", or "magician" does – what typical action (which brands him as belonging to one of these categories) is important and relevant for the analysis of it – before one can embark on the analysis ("value-relevance" in H. Rickert's sense)'.[78] Now the definition of, say, 'magician' undoubtedly furnishes an excellent example of the difficulties of concept-formation in the social sciences. Not merely will the 'characterising' value-judgements, if one wishes to call them that, involved in applying it be difficult and sometimes controversial, but its definition is bound, as Weber is quite right to emphasise, to raise the question of the 'cultural significance' of magic in the particular society under study. No closed definition of it is possible, and yet it has to be defined somehow or other before the sociologist, anthropologist or historian can start to hypothesise about its origins or functions in that society. But once again: what do these admitted difficulties have to do with '*value*-relevance'?

It is possible, of course, to define 'magic' in quite overtly evaluative terms, and if someone wishes to use it to mean quasi-medical, quasi-scientific or quasi-religious practices of which he disapproves then there is nothing to prevent him, just as 'rational' is sometimes used to mean practices of which the speaker approves

[78] *GAW*, p. 543 (Parsons, p. 107).

as opposed to 'irrational' practices of which he doesn't.[79] But this once detected is easy to dispose of. The more serious difficulties are serious precisely because they *aren't* merely the consequence of the intrusion of 'appraising' value-judgements. They are additionally intractable where the observer is studying a culture thoroughly alien to his own. But they arise to a greater or lesser degree in all sociological contexts. It is not simply that a term like 'magic' is, in Waissmann's celebrated expression, 'open-textured',[80] so that its users are faced with an unbounded prospect of successive 'characterising value-judgements' which they will have to apply. It is that in addition the decision which precedent to follow, or which alternative list of necessary and sufficient characteristics to prefer, has to be taken by reference at some level to the attitudes and beliefs of the members of the society whose practices are being categorised by the use of this term. This is a problem which is self-evidently peculiar to the social sciences, since it is only self-conscious beings who can have beliefs at all. But to persist in describing it as a matter of 'value-relevance' is simply punning on 'value'. To devote the attention which I have done to Weber's argument is, admittedly, to concede that the pun is a tempting one. But a successful diagnosis of what differentiates concept-formation in natural and in social science cannot but be obscured, and will perhaps be concealed altogether, if the temptation is not withstood. Only when this alleged dependence of sociological theory on the sociologist's values, as distinguished from his non-empirical presuppositions, has been disposed of will it be possible to see clearly where the significant difference between the sciences of man and the sciences of nature does indeed lie.

[79] Cf. Schopenhauer's remark in his *Eristische Dialektik* that the same ceremony may be described according to the rhetorical purposes of the speaker as an act of 'piety', of 'superstition' or (if the speaker neither approves nor disapproves) of 'public worship' (*Werke*, ed. Piper, VI, 414 quoted by Ch. Perelman and L. Olbrechts-Tyteca, *Traité de l'Argumentation* (Paris, 1958), I, 153; English translation by T. Bailey Saunders, *The Art of Controversy* (London, 1898), p. 25).

[80] Friedrich Waissmann, 'Verifiability', in Antony Flew, ed., *Logic and Language*, First Series (Oxford, 1963), pp. 117–44.

IV

There is still, however, one more hurdle to surmount before Weber's views about the logic of value-judgements can be left behind. Thus far, I have treated them in terms of his own distinction between 'value-freedom' on the one hand and 'value-relevance' on the other; and in so doing I have taken it for granted that whatever may be the difficulties about his view of the second he was at any rate right about the first. Indeed, many readers of the essay on 'The Meaning of "Value-freedom"' may have felt, as Halbwachs did, that Weber is making unnecessarily heavy weather of the obvious.[81] To this, however, there is the immediate answer that obvious though it may be, Weber was on the losing, not the winning, side at the closed meeting of the *Verein* for which the essay had first been written. Even if his view of the fact/value dichotomy is by now orthodox among the great majority both of social scientists and of philosophers, it is still not an orthodoxy which goes unchallenged. Weber may, therefore, need in some readers' eyes not merely to be defended against those who (like myself) regard his doctrine of value-relevance as resting on a confusion about 'values', but on the contrary to be criticised for failing to follow it up to the point of abandoning his prior insistence that 'ought' is logically separate from 'is'.

There are broadly three lines of attack which, if successfully pursued, would require Weber's claim that social science is 'value-free' to be abandoned. There is the frontal assault which is sometimes mounted on the alleged impossibility of deriving 'ought' from 'is'; there are the arguments of those moral philosophers now commonly labelled 'descriptivists' which purport to show that judgements of good and bad are not, after all, discretionary in the way that Weber for one believed; and there is the kind of so-called 'critical' sociological theory, deriving from the philosophical tradition rather of Hegel than of Kant, in which self-consciously evaluative propositions about human society are built into an

---

[81] Maurice Halbwachs, 'Max Weber, un homme, une œuvre', *Annales d'Histoire Economique et Sociale* I (1929), 84.

argument which claims at the same time to be susceptible of inter-subjective confirmation. These three categories are not exclusive, and there are several of Weber's critics who reject his doctrine of 'value-freedom' without falling neatly into one or another of them. But to understand, let alone to improve upon, Weber's philosophy of social science requires at least a brief exposition of the grounds on which he would – in my view, rightly – have rejected them.

To say that he would have rejected them is not to absolve Weber of the inconsistency in his own moral attitudes with which many of his commentators have charged him. Not only was the distinction between his academic judgements and his moral and political preferences less clear-cut than his doctrine of 'value-freedom' requires; but his moral and political preferences were themselves inconsistent, since he combined an ideology of passionate national-ism with a profound disdain for all other ideologists, nationalists included. But these criticisms *ad hominem* are no grounds for say-ing that the doctrine of 'value-freedom' is mistaken as a view of the logical relation, or lack of one, between the empirical generalisa-tions or causal hypotheses of social science and judgements of moral, aesthetic or political preference. Weber did, as we have seen, believe that social scientists' 'values' in some sense dictate the terms in which their hypotheses are formulated. But he did not believe, and was not thereby committed to believe, either that the truth or falsehood of social-scientific hypotheses is in any way a matter of 'values' or that any particular value-judgement is ever required by any given set of facts. Value-judgements must admit-tedly have regard to matters of fact to the extent that prescriptions derived from them may be impossible to execute or possible only at the cost of violating some other moral or political preference which the person in question has already expressed; but the choice of any single 'value' is free.

This '*wissenschaftsfreie Wertposition*', as Troeltsch was ironically to describe it,[82] reflects the joint influence of Nietzsche and of Kant. Not that Weber should, or would have been willing to be, labelled a 'neo-Kantian': already in the critique of Knies he speaks of 'Kant's "causality through freedom"' as the archetype of the kinds of 'metaphysical "culture-" and "personality"-theories' of which he disapproves.[83] But his attitude to Kant is more complicated than

[82] Quoted by Fleischmann, *op. cit.* p. 225.
[83] *GAW*, p. 62.

50

this suggests. He is a Kantian in matters of logic, at least; and in ethics, he is critical of Kant's categorical imperative not, as so many of Kant's commentators have been, on the grounds of its emptiness of substantive content – a criticism against which Kant can in any case be plausibly defended[84] – but on the grounds that such content as it has is not as compelling as Kant supposed. In the essay on 'Value-freedom' he says quite explicitly that it is false to suppose that Kant's axioms contain no 'substantive directions for evaluating action';[85] but he goes on to say that this is inadequate to resolve the choice of substantive ethical doctrines – or in a more typically Weberian phrase, 'decision for the ethically irrational conflict of different value-spheres'.[86] To be sure, any 'value-position' must be consistent. Indeed, I think Weber would have been willing to say that it must, in a term of more modern moral philosophy, be 'universalisable'. But there is a variety of irreconcilable moral positions all of which can be held as consistently as each other. In sexual morality, which is the example Weber uses, Kant's maxim has (he says) obvious substantive implications. But he then points out that it can quite well be turned on its head by someone who places a higher value on a relation in which the partners deliberately treat each other as means and not ends for such reasons as that it is more authentic, that it offers an escape from routine and convention, and so forth.[87] Someone who wants to, in other words, can always make a virtue of a vice, and the values of Nietszche or Baudelaire or Aleister Crowley or Jean Genet or Yukio Mishima are no less 'values' than the conventional code of conduct which they seek to deny. A value-judgement is untenable only if it is

[84] The *locus classicus* on which to base such a defence would be the essay 'On the Common Saying: "This may be True in Theory, but it does not Apply in Practice" ' of 1793. Weber, however, seems to have had in mind only the *Metaphysic of Morals* and *Critique of Practical Reason*.

[85] *GAW*, p. 491 (Shils, p. 16).

[86] The phrase is taken from a fragment among his papers which is reproduced by Baumgarten, *op. cit.* p. 400. It was apparently written in about 1912.

[87] *GAW*, p. 492 (Shils, p. 17). Cf. *GAW*, p. 246 (Shils, pp. 143–4) on the 'typical modern sexual philistine's' attitude to Goethe; and on political rather than sexual morality, see the well-known passage towards the end of 'Politics as a Vocation' where Weber echoes Macchiavelli's praise of those citizens of Florence who 'valued the greatness of their fatherland higher than the salvation of their souls' and contrasts the force of the papal interdict with (in Fichte's phrase) the 'cold approval' of the Kantian ethic (*GPS*, pp. 545–6 (G & M, p. 126)).

internally inconsistent, or incompatible with some other value-judgement simultaneously affirmed, or incompatible with known matters of fact. In other words, it can never be logically perverse to be morally perverse.

In practice, Weber himself is more than willing to bring arguments to bear against value-positions which are not his own. In particular, it is his repeated objection to the moral and political doctrines of the Left that they ignore the realities of politics and that they are therefore not merely utopian but irresponsible – a familiar complaint which is seldom as much a matter of fact as it is dressed up to appear. But having made this criticism, Weber does not deny to the revolutionary syndicalist or the pacifist or the anarchist or the Franciscan monk the right to adhere to his views. On the contrary, he sees this right as deriving precisely from the logical gulf between the matters of fact which can be established by science and the evaluative convictions which determine each man's choice of one rather than another conflicting 'demon'. When in both the lecture on 'Science as a Vocation' and the essay on 'Value-freedom' he commends Mill for the observation that 'if one proceeds from pure experience one comes to polytheism',[88] it is this inescapable need for decision in matters of value as opposed to fact which he has in mind.

The most common counter-argument to Weber's view consists in a claim that individual actions and, by extension, social states of affairs can be and are described, by social scientists and philosophers of Weber's persuasion as much as by anyone else, in terms of predicates which, although self-evidently evaluative, are applied in the same way and by the same sort of criteria as predicates which equally self-evidently are not. That this is commonly done in the writings of social scientists, and particularly historians, does not of course decide the issue any more than the entrenchment of our conventional vocabulary of responsibility and free will can decide the issue of causal explicability. But it is certainly true that

[88] *GAW*, p. 587 (G & M, p. 147); *GAW*, p. 493 (Shils, p. 17). This is one of the cases where Weber's English translators have been surprisingly careless, since both translate 'der alte Mill' as 'the elder Mill', thus turning an unmistakable reference to John Stuart Mill into a reference to his father, James. The more immediate debt which Weber acknowledges in addition to this rather grudging acknowledgement of Mill is to Gustav Radbruch's *Einführung in die Rechtswissenschaft*: see *GAW*, p. 485 nl (Shils, p. 10 n3).

we do habitually discuss such questions as whether Caesar's decisions were foolish, his motives cynical, or his way of life self-indulgent as though these were matters of fact, and except in philosophical discussion feel no particular unease in doing so. The argument centres, therefore, on the question whether or not there is, as Weber would maintain, an autonomous value-judgement shared, or presumed to be shared, by the social scientist and his readers which underlies the attribution to Caesar of the vices of foolishness, cynicism and self-indulgence or whether, on the contrary, the value-judgement that he was morally to be reprehended in these ways is entailed by the facts, once established as such, of Caesar's behaviour.

These two sides in the controversy have by now been entrenched in their positions for a good while, and the battleground has been fought over a number of times since Weber wrote without either having been forced into retreat. Without, however, attempting a résumé of twentieth-century moral philosophy, I think it is still plausible to suggest that much of the 'descriptivist' case could be conceded while leaving the fundamental assumptions underlying Weber's doctrine of 'value-freedom' intact. Weber's position is, in effect, that now labelled 'prescriptivist'[89] – that is, he holds not simply that to make a moral judgement is to commit oneself to acting if one can in certain ways, but also that any principle of conduct, however unexpected or 'irrational', may form the basis for such judgements. The objection which is, however, urged against prescriptivism is that in making moral judgements we quite self-consciously do something different from this: when we say that an action is good we do not mean that we are committing ourselves to performing it, but rather that the action, or way of life, or social policy in question has something about it which makes it a good thing to try to realise, whether we ourselves intend ever to do it or not. And the plausibility of the descriptivist case, accordingly, lies in the fact that we not only use 'evaluative' terms as we use ordinary, non-evaluative descriptive terms, but use them as though we *meant* them to function in the ordinary descriptive way and not as disguised imperatives.

Now if my reading of Weber is correct, he would never have been willing to concede the validity, and perhaps would even have

[89] See R. M. Hare, *The Language of Morals* (Oxford, 1952) and *Freedom and Reason* (Oxford, 1963).

denied the meaningfulness, of any moral argument resting on the presumption that we can be compelled to call an action or a state of affairs 'good' because of some set of empirical properties which it is shown to instantiate. But to preserve his doctrine of 'value-freedom' he needs only to be right in his conviction that whatever may determine our attribution of evaluative terms in personal or social contexts, it cannot be a matter of logic in the customary sense. Thus, it may be true that prescriptivism furnishes an inadequate account of moral reasoning and that the descriptivists are right to say that our standards of value do not and cannot simply emerge out of a vacuum. But it still doesn't follow that any one standard of valuation is ever required by the facts which social science has disclosed. As Weber puts it himself, 'the validity of a prescription [*praktischen Imperativs*] as a norm on the one hand and the truth-value of an empirical statement on the other lie at absolutely heterogeneous levels'.[90] Of course, it does so happen that there is quite widespread agreement on moral standards not only within but even between cultures: what social scientist, however wide his ethnographic experience, seriously expects to find a people who think it reprehensible *per se* to give help to a drowning friend or commendable *per se* to induce in one's children an addiction to heroin? But it is the essence of Weber's blend of Kant and Nietszche that we are not logically debarred from doing so. It is only once given agreement on a particular schedule of ends that it becomes natural within the culture in question to speak of certain actions as good ones, whether because they exemplify a personal attribute regarded as commendable or because they bring about what is held to be a desirable state of affairs. Value-judgements are of course inseparable from the factual description of whatever gives rise to them. But they rest on an autonomous premise that whatever it is is to be valued in the first place, so that to say, for example, that presidential '*Führerdemokratie*' is 'better' than a parliamentary system is to say that there are certain ends which the speaker holds to be those which a political system should fulfil and which (on his view of the facts) a presidential system will, and a parliamentary system will not, achieve. And in the same sort of way, to talk in sociological terms in which the descriptive and the evaluative are manifestly fused, such as 'murder' or 'exploitation', is to say that either in the social scientist's view (whatever the

[90] *GAW*, p. 487 (Shils, p. 12); cf. p. 225 (Shils, p. 123).

54

members of the culture may happen to hold) or, more often, in the view of the members of the culture in question (whatever the social scientist may happen to hold) certain categories of behaviour are to be approved or condemned.

At this point, the standard objection of the descriptivists is that this appeal to *oratio obliqua* is self-defeating: for if this is the correct analysis of moral terms, why is it not the correct analysis of scientific or logical terms? What is the difference between translating 'murder' into 'an act of killing which in their culture is believed to be wrong' and translating 'molecule' into 'a physical particle which in their culture is believed to be the smallest discrete portion into which a given substance can be divided without losing its chemical identity'? But Weber gives what is, in turn, the standard reply to this objection when he remarks that the distinctive characteristic of science and logic is precisely that (as he puts it) a Chinaman can be brought to accept their results so far as the data permit, whereas whatever we may say he can and does deny the moral ideals of our culture.[91] To be sure, the matter is not quite so simple as this. The discoveries of twentieth-century logicians have themselves undermined much of the certainty which attached to traditional logic in the eyes of Weber, as of Kant; the compulsion which theoretical as opposed to practical reason exercises has proved harder to demonstrate and justify than Weber would appear to have supposed; and the distinction between analytic and synthetic propositions has been subjected to powerful criticism, not always in ways compatible even with a radically modified version of Kant's. But even if the contrast which Weber draws in the critique of Knies between 'categorical' and 'phenomenological' certainty (*Evidenz*)[92] – in other words, between the intersubjectively acknowledged certainty attaching to logical or mathematical truths and the illusion of certainty attaching to the 'empathetic' insights of psychological intuitionism – is not so straightforward as he supposed, he is still entitled to contrast science with non-science. He is very ready to concede that non-scientific beliefs may be held with as much conviction as scientific; but this does not make them amenable in principle to intersubjective reconciliation in the same sort of way. The ethnographer who returns from an alien culture may have been made aware of the variability in human beliefs about matters

91 *GAW*, p. 155 (Shils, p. 58).
92 *GAW*, p. 116.

of fact no less than in beliefs about aesthetics or morality, and may even have stumbled upon a culture in which the capacity for scientific reasoning seems barely to be developed at all. But whereas this may cause him to be sceptical of the aesthetic or moral values of his own culture, it will hardly cause him to be sceptical of the assumptions of scientific method. Not that he will want to dogmatise about the content of science or, for that matter, of logic. But this is to say only that all scientific discoveries are provisional; it is not to say that we have discretion to accept or reject them of the kind that we have to accept or reject a moral code.

There is only one twentieth-century moral theory whose acceptance would be entirely incompatible with Weber's view of the nature of the divide between 'is' and 'ought', and that is ethical intuitionism itself, by which I mean the doctrine of G. E. Moore and his followers that there is a simple, non-natural, *sui generis* property for which the name 'goodness' stands. Weber, of course, would have been wholly out of sympathy with the substantive content of Moore's *Principia Ethica* (which he might have read, but as far as I am aware did not): Moore's parochial and even cloistered view of the moral life, in which the cultivation of personal relationships and the appreciation of beauty are the ends held chiefly to embody the good, could hardly be more remote from Weber's vision of an unceasing struggle between antagonistic convictions and the perpetual necessity for personal choice between an 'ethic of responsibility' and an 'ethic of ultimate ends'. But whatever the merits or demerits of either Moore's or Weber's practical views, I think it can safely be said that intuitionism of Moore's kind is no longer held to be a seriously plausible account of moral judgement. If intuitionism needs to be taken more seriously than Weber was willing to do, this is only in the sense that any ethical system claiming to demonstrate that there are good reasons for behaving in some rather than other ways is appealing to our *a priori* judgements. But what follows? Only that there may be more constraints on moral decision than Weber allows. Even if there are, after all, Kantian axioms which compel rational men, however defined, to acknowledge an obligation to act in certain ways, they do not entail adherence to any one specific way of life and they do not relate as mathematics and logic do to the practice of science. They are still as independent of the discoveries of science as the wider range of 'practical imperatives' which Weber allowed as possible choices;

and conversely, as Weber put it in the editorial of 1904, 'An empirical science cannot teach anyone what he should, but only what he can and – under certain circumstances – what he wants to do'.[93] Even if Weber's moral philosophy is demonstrably fallacious, the 'value-freedom' of science, and therefore of social science, is inviolate.

It remains true that social scientists disagree in a way that natural scientists or mathematicians do not. As Wittgenstein said, and before Wittgenstein Hobbes, mathematicians don't come to blows; whereas how (Weber asks) can a Catholic and a Freemason ever be brought to share a common *Wertung* of religious history?[94] To draw this contrast, however, is only to point out again that, as no one denies, social scientists, unlike mathematicians, deal with topics about which different people do indeed hold incompatible moral and political values; and this, so far from showing that the gap between facts and values is not as wide as Weber thinks, merely reinforces his argument that wholly irreconcilable values are compatible with the acceptance of the same set of facts. It may be said that apart from matters of value, the Freemason and the Catholic will differ over what *constitutes* the facts: as Weber readily concedes, the Catholic's history will include explanations in terms such as 'miracle' and 'revelation' which find no place in the Freemason's account. But the freedom of the Catholic to believe in a doctrine of divine revelation does not undermine the autonomy of science any more than does his freedom to apportion praise and blame in accordance with standards which the Freemason will be bound to reject. If theology is ever to modify science, it will have to do so on science's, not on theology's, terms: to the extent that the rise of Christianity can be explained without reference to supernatural influences it must be, and the believer can, as Weber emphasises, accept such explanation without being untrue to his faith.[95] A religious, political, aesthetic or moral persuasion is compatible with anything which empirical science may disclose because, and only because, such persuasions derive from premises which are logically independent of those which underlie empirical science.

It is, of course, the case that in practice the logical separation of fact from value is frequently blurred. Not only is it deliberately

[93] *GAW*, p. 151 (Shils, p. 54).
[94] *GAW*, p. 586 (G & M, p. 146).
[95] *GAW*, p. 587 (G & M, p. 147).

blurred by those social scientists who believe, like Treitschke and Mommsen and many since, that it ought to be, but it is also blurred by many who claim, and appear to believe, that the propositions which they put forward are morally and politically neutral when in fact they are not. In such cases, the necessary disentanglement is sometimes difficult to achieve. But it follows from the charge that a piece of social-scientific writing is *not* value-free that it can in principle be made so by identifying the evaluative terms within it and substituting for them alternative terms with the same extension but a different evaluative content. This may still leave open a dispute about the 'characterising value-judgements' which underlie the application of these terms. But as I remarked in the previous section, these are not value-judgements in the sense with which Weber was concerned. It can happen that a social scientist's decision to use or not to use some particular 'characterising' term is dictated by his 'appraisive' values: he may wish to withhold, say, the attribution of a term like 'democracy' or 'slavery' or 'revolution' to some given state of affairs not because he can give a list of necessary and sufficient conditions which it fails to exemplify but because to do so would involve the assimilation of societies of which he approves to societies of which he doesn't. But his factual claims about it are not going to be affected by this: or if they are, then the claims were not, although they may have been dressed up to be, factual. The point is effectively the same as in the example of 'class' which I discussed in the context of 'value-relevance', and if it holds there it must hold *a fortiori* for cases where an unmistakably evaluative term appears in a social-scientific text. Indeed, the claim that social, as opposed to natural, science is necessarily infected with judgements of value is, as has often enough been remarked, self-defeating. However frequently social science is in fact so infected, to say that it is entails that the infection can be diagnosed, and to say that it can be diagnosed entails that it can in principle be cured. It cannot always be cured in practice, as Weber's failure to convince his opponents in the *Verein* already shows. But the only way that Weber's doctrine of 'value-freedom' can actually be controverted is by an effective demonstration that matters of fact and of values are not logically distinguishable after all.

There remain still other senses in which it is sometimes said that value-judgements enter into the practice of social science, but they are of even less relevance to Weber's argument. I have already

58

mentioned two which he is at pains to dismiss himself – the value-judgements implied first, in choosing one problem rather than another, and second, in seeking to arrive at correct findings rather than incorrect ones. But neither is relevant to the differences, whatever they may be, between natural and social science; and no more are any other of the ways in which the practice of science is sometimes said to involve value-judgements. The statistician, for example, who decides on a significance level below which he will reject the null hypothesis or decides to plot his data on logarithmic paper or to rotate the axes in a factor analysis is sometimes said in some sense of the phrase to be 'making a value-judgement'. But this has nothing whatever to do with the problems with which Weber was concerned. It can perhaps be said that Weber himself never gives an entirely satisfactory definition of what he does regard as the proper sense of 'value-judgement': the nearest he gets to it is at the opening of the essay on 'Value-freedom' where he says that *Wertungen* should be understood to mean '"practical" evaluations as either reprehensible or commendable of some manifestation subject to the influence of our actions'.[96] But unclear though this may be, it does bring out the point that the whole question of 'values' in social science is about the judgements which attach to human action and its consequences for human beings. The thesis of 'value-freedom' is not a thesis about the criteria of scientific practice, but about the irrelevance to the validity of scientific hypotheses of the standards by which the social scientist himself judges human conduct. For this reason, it cannot arise at all in the sciences of nature. But from the fact that it arises in the sciences of man it does not follow that these sciences are therefore 'infected' by values. On the contrary: from the fact that we can see where and how *Wertungen can* intrude into the practice of social science, it follows that we can discount them; and it is only what is left after this has been done that can be called social science at all.

This is still not all that needs to be said about the problem of values in social science, since they are themselves one of the areas of human behaviour which social science sets out to study, and this, as we shall see, raises difficult problems about the construction and use of the descriptive terms required for the purpose. But it is, I hope, all that needs to be said about the 'value-freedom' of social science itself. Whatever the difficulties of other kinds involved in

[96] *GAW*, p. 475 (Shils, p. 1).

either describing values or assessing them, and however mistaken may have been Weber's ideas about resolving them, his view of the logical independence of facts and values would have to be directly controverted on its own ground before he could be required to concede that the validity of a social scientist's findings can either entail or be entailed by his judgements of value. Indeed, it is a direct consequence of Weber's view that he could himself be entirely wrong both in his social science and in his moral and political philosophy without his case for the value-freedom of social science being in the smallest degree impugned.

V

Of the three principal errors with which I said at the beginning that Weber should be charged, I have now disposed as best I can of the first – his confusion between theoretical presuppositions and judgements of value. But the second – his misconception of the role of causal laws in the explanation of human behaviour – has been dealt with only to the extent that it is directly linked to the first. Weber's view that there must be some starting-point from which a causal enquiry is developed and that without such a starting-point the enquiry would be 'steering without a compass on a boundless sea'[97] is, as we have seen, perfectly correct. But his concomitant contention that causal explanation is 'guided by value-analysis' follows only in a trivial and misleading sense of 'value'. The more important question is whether there is still a difference between causal explanation in social and in natural science although in both cases the investigator has first to have formulated his hypotheses by reference to what happens to puzzle or interest him. The answer must, as we have also seen, be yes to the extent that causal explanations of human action have reference to the motives of the agent without, however, directly appealing to lawlike generalisations in which categories of motives feature as subject terms. But it is possible to agree with this answer as far as it goes while denying not merely that 'values' have anything to do with it but also that laws of some kind don't. I have already suggested that Weber's denial of the applicability of general laws in the social sciences arose in part from his mistaken view of psychology. But if his view of psychology is a wrong one, what alternative view of it is right? To correct Weber, it will be necessary not simply to demonstrate that he was inconsistent in denying that human history can be explained by reference to laws while insisting at the same time on the universal applicability of cause and effect, but also to say where the laws are to be found which do after all underlie the explanation of unique historical sequences of meaningful human action.

It could perhaps be argued that Weber needs to be corrected at

[97] *GAW*, p. 251 (Shils, p. 149).

a still more fundamental level, since his view of 'cause' itself has by now an undeniably old-fashioned air. But this is not so serious a failing as it may seem. It is true that just as Weber's view, which he shares with Kant, of the self-evidence of the truths of mathematics and logic would have had to be modified if he had lived to witness the revolution in these topics effected by Gödel and others, so he would have had to modify his, and Kant's, view of the physical world in the light of the revolution effected by quantum mechanics and the relativity theories of Einstein. But his rather restricted and even mechanistic assumptions about causal relations can be suitably enlarged without affecting the main point at issue.[98] Indeed, he is already less mechanistic in his historical writings than might appear from some of his methodological writings and in particular some of his strictures against historical materialism. He is very well aware of the importance of interdependence and feedback, and although he sometimes talks in such terms as to imply a view of history as (in Bury's term) successive 'concatenations',[99] the reciprocal influence of different social institutions is fundamental to his own account of historical evolution. It is true that he devotes little attention to explanations of the kind which are not strictly causal in the conventional sense: his occasional references to linguistics, for example, do not and could hardly be expected to envisage the explanatory potential of structural as opposed to historical analysis in the manner of Chomsky. But for the purposes of this essay, it will be enough to take him as concerned with the analysis of causal explanation in the broadest sense. The problem is then to put right his view of the relation of causal explanation to laws in the social as opposed to the natural sciences.

The correction required is in fact a smaller one than the discus-

[98] I claim no competence to start talking about the philosophical implications of the overthrow of classical physics. But whatever difficulties surround twentieth-century notions of indeterminacy, even the layman can recognise that the quantum principle does not deny the observed lawfulness of the natural world but, on the contrary, furnishes a better explanation of it than the classical principles. A very helpful discussion by a philosopher of both natural and social science is David Hawkins, *The Language of Nature* (San Francisco, 1964), ch. 7.

[99] See e.g. his reference to causal 'links' and 'chains' in the essay on Meyer (*GAW*, p. 269 n3 (Shils, p. 167 n35)). By contrast, however, his odd-sounding remark that, as translated by Parsons, *PE*, p. 27, 'we treat here only one side of the causal chain' should be rendered 'we investigate here only one aspect of the causal relation' (*GAR* I, 12: '*Hier wird also nur der einen Seite der Kausalbeziehung nachgegangen*').

sion up to this point might appear to suggest. Indeed, Weber is so very nearly right about the logic of explanation in history and sociology that much subsequent discussion of it, whether by social scientists or philosophers, marks a regression rather than an advance. Weber is, I believe, right in almost all that he says about the problems both of the subjective nature of social action and of the uniqueness of historical events; it is only his misconception of the relevance to sociological explanation of 'values' on the one hand and 'psychology' on the other which render his account untenable as it stands. Before trying to put it right, therefore, it may be as well if I cite his two main arguments, both of which are perfectly sound.

The first is his argument about 'adequate causation' (*adequäte Verursachung*). This is not to do with his distinction between 'causal adequacy' and 'adequacy at the level of meaning', but with the sense in which 'a', or even 'the', cause of a particular historical event can be specified. Its significance is twofold. In the first place, what constitutes 'adequate' causation depends on the particular contrast which the investigator wishes to draw between what has in fact occurred and some other sequence which would have resulted if the 'cause' in question had been absent: Weber may have been wrong to say that 'causal imputation' is a matter of 'values', but he was quite right to say that it is dependent on context. In the second place, the formulation of the explanation proceeds by a successive elimination of possible alternatives: it is never possible to demonstrate conclusively that 'the' cause which is finally cited was the decisive one,[100] but only that it could have been decisive and since every other plausible candidate has been shown not to furnish an adequate explanation it is to be presumed that indeed it was. For both these reasons, Weber is rightly contemptuous of any attempt to construct a 'monocausal' sociological theory: in the critique of Stammler, he says that to claim that everything in social life can be traced either to a spiritual or, for that matter, an economic factor is as foolish as to claim that 'in the last analysis' it is all to be explained by phrenology or sunspots or digestive disorders.[101] To rephrase the point with the help of terms borrowed

[100] The implication that 'values' therefore enter into historical explanation is the more surprising since Weber elsewhere acknowledges that 'precise reduction to individual causal components' is equally rare in natural science and the study of human action (*W & G* I, 118 (Parsons, p. 317)).
[101] *GAW*, pp. 298–9.

from a more recent philosopher of social science, sociological (and therefore, as Weber acknowledged, idiographic) explanation requires first the specification of the 'contrast state' and then the demonstration that a particular condition was, as far as the evidence is able to show, 'contingently sufficient' to bring about the actual state of affairs observed as opposed to the state of affairs which, given only the same background of antecedent necessary conditions, would have obtained without it.[102] If, therefore, Weber is taken as saying that sociological explanation proceeds without overt reference to articulated general laws, he is entirely correct.

The second of his arguments which is sound is one which I have mentioned already – his argument that actions consciously done for reasons are not thereby removed from the scope of causal explanation. It is true that his discussion of the relation between motives and intentions on the one hand and actions on the other is not entirely clear. But in practice, this does not much matter. The fact that so much of human action does follow ascertainable and consistent rules is a convenience which, as Weber points out, enables the practising sociologist to shortcut many of his explanations of particular sequences of actions and events. But then it has still, for Weber, to be empirically demonstrated how far the agents in question did follow the 'ideal-typical' rules which the sociologist seeks to apply to them. What is more, even where the sociologist is right in his diagnosis of the agent's reasoning he has still to show how it comes about that this sequence of reasoning, and not some other, was followed. There are admittedly no known laws which would make it possible infallibly to predict in advance the way in which any particular agent will in fact reason. But the agents' 'decision-schemes', as they would nowadays be called, are not on that account uncaused, and they are accordingly not inexplicable in principle. Some actions, it is true, are incapable of being 'interpreted and understood by direct analogy with the constitution of our own minds'[103] in the way that the sociologist or historian is

102 See Michael Scriven, 'Causes, Connections and Conditions in History', in William H. Dray, ed., *Philosophical Analysis and History* (New York, 1966), pp. 254–5 and 'Review of Nagel, *The Structure of Science*', *Review of Metaphysics* XVII (1964), 408. The same idea can be found in Mill, as Weber, despite his preceding criticism of him, acknowledges at the very end of the note which I have just cited (above, n99) on 'causal chains'.

103 *GAW*, p. 277 (Shils, p. 175).

used to: Weber's favourite example is the conduct of Frederick William IV of Prussia. But this is only to say that such actions have to be explained in clinical or psychopathological terms rather than the terms in which historians or sociologists are versed.[104] There is in this sense a difference between 'rational' and 'irrational' actions; but it is a difference not between the explicable and the inexplicable but between one sort of causal explanation and another. It goes without saying that at either end of the spectrum there are many actions which in practice defy the researches of even the most skilful and patient investigator. I have already quoted from *Economy and Society* both the remark that definitive causal analysis is rarely attainable even in natural science and the passage where Weber points out the dangers of 'imaginary experiments'. In this passage, he in fact goes on to say that 'control of a subjective understanding can be achieved with relative accuracy only in the regrettably small number of special cases suitable for psychological experiment'.[105] But actions are not therefore inherently immune to explanation, whether because they have no discernable rationale or, on the contrary, because the agent's reasoning is too elaborate or elliptical to be readily grasped. Weber is quite right to stand on its head the Idealists' argument that human actions must be inexplicable to the extent that they are 'freely' willed: it is, as he pointed out in his criticism of Roscher and Knies, precisely because people do choose their courses of action rather than leaving them to chance that the observer can so often reconstruct their antecedents by analogy with his own experience. Whether, or in what contexts, a person's reasons should themselves be described as a, or the, cause of his actions is not a question on which a definitive pronouncement is required. The important point is that no actions have to be regarded as causally inexplicable in principle, however difficult the explanation may be and however many kinds of antecedent conditions the request for an explanation may in context require.

These two precepts about explanation can be abundantly illustrated from Weber's own work. His account of the development of European capitalism, in particular, rests on the specification of a particular conjunction of antecedent conditions ranging from

---

[104] *GAW*, p. 78.

[105] *GAW*, p. 535 (Parsons, p. 97) cited above, p. 25 n38. At the same time, however, Weber willingly recognises that 'for the purposes of theory it is useful to work with extreme examples' (*W & G* I, 196 (Rheinstein, p. 36)).

double-entry book-keeping to urbanisation. But we are again up against the difficulty that an example chosen from Weber's own work may lead into substantive controversies which for the purposes of this essay I wish to bypass. I have therefore chosen as a less contentious and better manageable example the discussion by a later economic historian of a problem of very much the kind with which Weber was concerned. It does not matter for our purposes here whether the explanation put forward is in fact correct; for all I know, it has been shown by still more recent research to be mistaken. Its usefulness is that it clearly and briefly illustrates how the vindication of an 'adequate' cause characteristically rests on the postulation of an 'ideal type', the imputation of motives to the agents in question and the specification of the 'contingently sufficient' conditions which resulted in the occurrence of the events to be explained.

The example is the account given by Postan of the transition from slavery to dependent smallholding to wage labour in English mediaeval agriculture.[106] In any such example, there is of course the difficulty that the evidence is slender and uncertain. But this means only that Postan's findings, like those of any scientific enquiry, are susceptible to the possibility of subsequent correction; it does not affect the methodological issue. Postan's argument, very summarily, is that the creation of serving smallholdings was the obvious way for the lord of empty lands suitable for agricultural occupation at once to improve the productivity of his demesnes and to safeguard the supply of servants. The decisive influence was not the teachings of the Church, although these may have had some small effect in motivating individual believers to perform acts of manumission. It was rather the physical separation of the *bovarius*, unlike the slave, from the lord's *curia*. The dependent smallholder was able, as the slave was not, to set up a family and he thus had at the same time a strong inducement to exploit his holding to the full. Once this practice became widespread, however, it led to the proliferation of tenancies, the overabundance of population and a rise in prices; and this in turn made the increasing use of hired labour both possible and profitable.

The first thing to notice about this account is that it rests jointly on 'material' causes and on the motives of economic 'rationality'

106 M. M. Postan, 'The Famulus: the Estate Labourer in the xiith and xiiith Centuries', *Economic History Review Supplements*, 2 (Cambridge, n.d.).

attributed to the typical lord of an underexploited demesne. It is incidentally worth remarking that Postan's emphasis on the domestic situation of slaves parallels that which Weber gave to it in his own discussion of Imperial Rome: Weber saw the key to Rome's failure to develop economically in the contradiction between a mode of production resting increasingly on slavery and a mode of social relations which denied a normal family to slaves. But from the point of view of the logic of historical explanation, it is the parallel between an argument like Postan's and Weber's methodological precepts which is striking. Postan's formulation of his chosen problem is of course dictated by his particular interests as an economic historian of the period, and to Weber his 'attachment of cultural significance' to one rather than another sequence of causes and effects would no doubt be a case of 'relevance to values'. But it is possible while rejecting this claim for the reasons I have already given still to accept that the role of both 'idealisation' and 'adequate causation' in the example is as Weber lays down. Postan specifies the contrast between slavery, dependent smallholding and wage labour which furnishes the framework for an enquiry into the causes of the successive transition from one to the other during the period in question. He sets out the background of necessary conditions without which the possibility of the transition would not have arisen. He considers but rejects the hypothesis that ideological causes could be adequate to account for it. Instead, he shows what, given the material background, would be the 'rational' decision of a lord wishing to maximise the profitability of his lands. He does not suggest either that every lord was in fact so motivated or that those who were adopted in every detail the policies which would conform to the 'ideal type' of profit maximisation. But he does suggest that if this *were* the motive of a sufficient number, it *would* provide an 'adequate' cause of what requires to be explained; and since there seems to be sufficient evidence to show that this was indeed the case, this explanation is presumably entitled to stand for as long as no suggested alternative which might have been contingently sufficient to bring about the observed transition can more plausibly be advanced. It is, as always, open to the Idealist critic to question whether the motives of the twelfth-century lords should be described as 'causes' as well as, or instead of, 'reasons'. But in practice, the imputation of motives has to merge into an unmistakably causal narrative. The best answer to such a critic is perhaps

Weber's own in the editorial of 1904: 'From our point of view, "purpose" is the notion of a result which is the cause of an action; and it must be taken into account just as must any cause which produces or can produce a significant result. Its particular significance consists only in the fact that we not only describe human action but also can and wish to understand it.'[107]

There is, of course, a further feature of the example which I have chosen which conforms to Weber's analysis of historical explanation, and that is its lack of reference to general laws. But although it is perfectly true that historians' explanations, and even the most successful of them, seldom if ever make overt reference to laws, this is so for a different reason than the one which Weber holds. It is here, and only here, that a correction needs to be made to what he says about 'adequate causation'. The reason for which historians, sociologists and anthropologists fail to cite general laws in support of their idiographic explanations of human action is not that there aren't such laws, but that we don't know precisely what these laws are and (more surprisingly, perhaps) do not need to be able to state them in order to test one idiographic explanation against another. Weber is entirely right about the impossibility of laws of history as such. But he is wrong to conclude from this that there are no laws of any other kind to which historical explanation implicitly, if not explicitly, appeals.

His difficulty arises partly from his view of natural science which, as I have already remarked, was a rather restricted one by twentieth-century standards, and partly from his understandable tendency to view the issues involved in the terms of the arguments between the Idealists and Positivists of his period. To be sure, he was right not only in his scepticism about historical laws but in his recognition that sociology (or history or anthropology) are 'unrestricted' sciences: the historian of the Black Death or the spread of syphilis, although he is interested in the social rather than the bacteriological causes and effects associated with it, has still to rest his account on a presumptive acceptance of the truths of a number of sciences other than his own.[108] What Weber fails to recognise, however, is

[107] *GAW*, p. 183 (Shils, p. 83).
[108] See *GAW*, pp. 54, 99; and cf. e.g. the remark of Marc Bloch in *The Historian's Craft* (tr. Putnam; Manchester, 1954), p. 68 that 'few sciences, I believe, are forced to use so many dissimilar tools at the same time'. The use of the term 'unrestricted' in this context is borrowed from Pantin, *op. cit.*

that history or sociology are not only historical and 'unrestricted' but also applied sciences. I mean this not in the sense that they are applied (although they may be) to some practical social purpose, but in the sense that they are parasitic on the laws of others: historical, or sociological, explanation rests on the presumptive application of laws of psychology, just as biological explanation rests on the presumptive application of the laws of physiology and biochemistry, and geological explanation on the presumptive application of the laws of physics.

Weber's failure to recognise this may seem doubly surprising in view of his insistence both on the universality of cause and effect and on the reducibility in extensional terms of statements about collectivities to statements about individuals. But the fact remains that he did fail to recognise it. The discussion of 'objective possibility and adequate causation' in the critique of Meyer comes very close to it: in the example which Weber uses of a mother explaining to her husband how she has come, contrary to her usual practice, to strike their child, he seems clearly to acknowledge that the explanation presupposes the truth of what we would nowadays call the 'counterfactual conditional';[109] and this should in turn imply the truth of a lawlike generalisation justifying the account of what would have happened (or not) in the contrast case. But Weber leads the discussion instead into questions about chance and probability on the one hand and significance in terms of the historian's interests on the other. He fights shy of the complete agreement with the Positivists, the 'Classical' (as against the 'Historical') economists, and Mill's *System of Logic* to which his own argument might seem to be leading him because of his conviction that reference to general laws can only ever be contributory to, and never constitutive of, historical explanation. This, as I pointed out earlier, remained his position even though he came to modify the more extreme assertions which he made in the editorial of 1904. In the second part of the critique of Roscher and Knies, he already puts it more moderately by saying that 'history employs general concepts and "laws" where these are useful for the attribution of cause in an individual case, but it does not itself set out to construct such laws'[110] – which is perfectly true inasmuch as history is not a

---

[109] *GAW*, pp. 279–80 (Shils, pp. 177–8).
[110] *GAW*, pp. 90–1.

producer but only a consumer of laws. The trouble is, however, that Weber draws from it the implication that there is therefore something other than 'reference to laws' by which historical explanation has to be justified.

In the 1904 editorial, he considers directly the possibility that psychology might 'create a sort of "chemistry" of the psychological foundations of social life'.[111] But he is entirely unequivocal in his rejection of it as a foundation for social science. He does not wish to say that such a thing is impossible in principle. But he does wish to say that even if it were to be achieved it would not yield 'knowledge of causal interrelations' of the kind which the social scientist is after: it would constitute only the accomplishment of 'a useful preliminary task'.[112] This, again, is true in one way but altogether false in another. Knowledge of psychological laws, wherever they were to be found, would admittedly not yield these explanations *by themselves* any more than knowledge of the laws of physics yields by itself the explanation of the particular phenomena studied by the geologist. But at the same time, no further justification for the historian's or geologist's explanation is required than the specification of certain known or even purely presumptive laws from the underlying disciplines which are relevant to it and the 'idiographic' demonstration that, given the antecedent conditions of the particular case, these laws are 'adequate' in Weber's own sense to account for the actual occurrence of the chosen explanandum. Thus in the example which I took from Postan, although the explanation does not rest on direct 'reference to laws', whether of economic development or of the motives and purposes of landlords, it does and must nonetheless rest on the tacit assumption that there are lawlike generalisations which vindicate the counterfactual conditionals implicit in the specification of the contrast case. This statement has, admittedly, to be qualified to the degree that purely random influences can affect the course of historical events, whether human or only physical, as Weber rightly points out.[113] But the claim that

111 *GAW*, p. 173 (Shils, p. 75).
112 *GAW*, p. 174 (Shils, p. 75); cf. *GAW*, pp. 112–13.
113 In his discussion of 'objective possibility and adequate causation', he considers the throw of a die and correctly remarks that although it is true that the outcome is causally determined by the precise form of the throw, it is quite impossible to formulate an empirical generalisation to cover it; we can generalise only in terms of the calculus of probabilities. See *GAW*, pp. 284–5 (Shils, pp. 182–3).

the perception of their economic interests by twelfth-century lords *was* contingently sufficient in context to bring about the transition from slavery to dependent smallholding to wage labour presupposes that there is, among the innumerable others which are relevant to the case, a lawlike generalisation such as guarantees that the connection would hold, *ceteris paribus*, in any other case. As Weber himself says, quoting from Schopenhauer, 'causality is not a cab that one can retain or dismiss at will'.[114]

Weber's conviction that psychological laws, if found, would be no more directly relevant to the practice of history or sociology than discoveries about nutrition or ageing or inherited differences of aptitude or character seems to derive in part from the desire which, in his very different way, Weber shares with Durkheim, not to allow the autonomy of sociology to be infringed by disciplines which are no more than ancillary to it. Sociology and history may, on Weber's argument, require the 'understanding' of human behaviour in a sense obviously inapplicable to biological or physical science; but even '*verstehende*' sociology is emphatically not a part of psychology.[115] Yet he could have conceded the dependence of sociology and history on the presumptive laws of psychology without thereby surrendering their autonomy. The geologist does not abdicate from his specialism because of his dependence on physics or the biologist from his because of his dependence on physiology and biochemistry. All the historical and therefore open-ended sciences, whether physical, biological or social, share both the same inability to predict accurately in advance and the same lack of autonomous general laws by comparison with classical mechanics. But this does not mean that they do not constitute legitimate specialisms or that they are incapable of explaining the 'historical individuals', in Weber's phrase,[116] with which they are concerned. It means only that their explanations require the implicit backing

---

[114] *GAW*, p. 77; and cf. his later echo of the same remark applied to historical materialism in the lecture on 'Politics as a Vocation' (*GPS*, p. 545 (G & M, p. 125)).

[115] *GAW*, p. 432.

[116] This term, borrowed from Rickert, is quite frequently used in the methodological essays, but the best definition of it is in the *Protestant Ethic* where Weber describes it as 'a complex of related elements in historical reality which we bring together into a conceptual whole from the standpoint of their cultural significance': see *GAR* I, 30 (Parsons, *PE*, p. 47). Weber's examples range from 'Greek culture' (*GAW*, p. 122) to *Das Kapital* (*GAW*, p. 253 (Shils, p. 151)).

of one or more sciences which are unhistorical and 'pure' relative to them.

Among the many sciences, however, on which sociological explanations may rest as their context requires, psychology must be conceded to stand in a special relation of its own towards them. I have suggested that Weber might have been expected to recognise this in view of his insistence that the fundamental subject-matter of the social sciences is the self-conscious actions of individual persons. But since he did not believe that there have been or will ever be discovered general laws which govern these actions, it was perhaps natural that he should relegate psychology to the role of furnishing clinical explanations of 'irrational' action in the same sort of way that physiology furnishes explanations of bodily disorders which may be of importance in some particular sequence of historical causes and effects. Had he recognised that it is a characteristic feature of idiographic explanations that the laws on which they must somewhere rest need not be fully stated or even fully known, he would perhaps have been willing to accord to psychology a less restricted status. Such a recognition, indeed, would not only have modified his ambivalent attitude to psychology, or social psychology, but would have removed the apparent inconsistency between his adherence to the fundamental tenets of Positivism and his simultaneous concessions to the 'Historical' school of political economy. But he never envisaged that he might be right about the impossibility of laws of human behaviour of the form of laws of mechanics and yet wrong about the impossibility of any laws at all which could furnish the observed regularities of human behaviour with theoretical grounding.

A more detailed analogy between sociological and biological explanation may be illuminating at this point, provided that any hint of 'social Darwinism' is rejected as firmly as would be done by Weber himself. Biological, like sociological, evolution is the outcome of complex concatenations of circumstances which successively determine the constraints within which future evolution will be bound. It is a one-way, open-ended process which cannot be predicted by reference to any kind of developmental law. But at the same time, particular changes can be satisfactorily explained in retrospect by reference to the observable features of the environment and the mechanism of genetic transformation. In the biological, unlike the sociological, case we now know in considerable

72

detail the manner in which teleonomic changes in species result from environmental pressure for selection and a process of random mutation. But it is worth noticing that a correct account of the effect of the environment on a given species could be given even without a knowledge of the genetics and the underlying biochemistry: Darwin himself, after all, was right about natural selection although wrong about inheritance. We are at present very far indeed from a knowledge of psychology comparable to our knowledge of genetics; despite the advances which have been made since Weber's time in neurophysiology, experimental psychology and control systems theory, our understanding of the prodigious complexity of the human brain is still no more than rudimentary. But it is possible for the sociologist or historian to advance convincing idiographic explanations of human actions, once observed, without his being able to specify the laws governing the psychological mechanisms which underlie them. All that is needed is for him to be able to say first, that there must *be* a mechanism which makes possible what is known sometimes (although we cannot say precisely under what conditions) to be the correlation between an operationally definable psychological state and the item of behaviour observed;[117] and second, that the necessary and sufficient conditions can be presumed to have been fulfilled in the given case because any other plausible alternative is incompatible with the evidence.

The analogy between sociological and biological explanation thus extends to the logical structure of idiographic explanations which rest on specifying some one improbable conjunction of circumstances which, when taken together, appear to have accounted for the occurrence of the explanandum. Since the case may well be unique, it may seem particularly irrelevant to look for general laws under which it might be subsumed. But compare a biologist seeking to explain the origin of life itself with Weber's own attempt to explain the origin of industrial capitalism. The biologist's account will involve a specification of the way in which it must, in the light of our knowledge of the laws of chemistry, have come about that amino acids were produced in a 'primitive sea' containing ammonia,

---

[117] There is therefore (as in the biological case) a negative corollary that 'it is sufficient to disconfirm a functional account of the behaviour of an organism to show that its nervous system is incapable of assuming states manifesting the functional characteristics that account requires'; see Jerry A. Fodor, 'Explanations in Psychology', in Max Black, ed., *Philosophy in America* (London, 1965), p. 176.

methane and water vapour but no oxygen.[118] If, having justified this account, he can go on to spell out the way in which a succession of possible chemical reactions could, and therefore must, have brought about the formation of adenine and the other components of deoxyribonucleic acid, he will have given a provisional but strongly persuasive explanation of the evolution of self-reproducing molecules. Similarly, Weber's account of the manner and the sequence in which the emergence of formally free labour, cities within national states, technology resting on science rather than philosophy, rational accounting, stable currency, private accumulations of capital, joint-stock ownership, legal codes based on the concept of citizenship, and a religious as opposed to a magical ethic for the conduct of life led to the emergence of industrial capitalism in Western Europe rests on the presumption of psychological (as well as other) regularities of cause and effect based not, as in the biological case, on any experimental evidence but on the sort of quasi-experimental comparisons which are all that the social sciences can normally provide.

It may be objected at this point that my account of sociological, or historical, explanation, although doing justice to Weber's recognition that causal regularities don't simply break off when we move from nature to culture, has nonetheless bypassed his explicit refusal to allow social-psychological research any role beyond that of improving our 'understanding' of institutions.[119] If, therefore, Weber is corrected along the lines which I am proposing, what happens to his doctrine of 'understanding' itself and his view of the part played by motives in the explanation of human action? The answer to this, however, lies in his own assertion that the difference between the 'inner' and 'outer' aspect of human action is only a

---

[118] Sceptics may here bring forward an argument, analogous to the Idealist argument against the possibility of historical knowledge, to the effect that we cannot claim to know what went on in the primitive sea unless we can claim somehow to have observed it directly: what licences the inference from observations of allegedly similar conditions in the laboratory to conclusions about what actually happened millennia ago? But this is rather like saying, to borrow an example of Hilary Putnam's, that 'we would have to *heat cadmium on the sun* before we could say that the regularity upon which we base our spectrographic analysis of sunlight had been verified'; see his 'Brains and Behaviour', in R. J. Butler, ed., *Analytical Philosophy*, Second Series (Oxford, 1965), p. 16. Such arguments need to be taken no more seriously by the practising researcher than Croce's.

[119] *GAW*, p. 189 (Shils, p. 89).

difference in the accessibility of the requisite evidence.[120] Once it is accepted that Weber is not really talking about 'empathy' in the Idealists' sense according to which the historian is supposed to 'recreate' the experience of his subjects,[121] but only about 'understanding' in the harmless sense that one must understand the meaning of someone's words or thoughts before being able to explain them, it then becomes possible to reconcile his doctrine of '*verstehen*' with an acceptance of the relevance to the social sciences of presumptive psychological laws. There is, it may be said, a sense in which a basis of shared experience is presupposed by the sharing of a common language: a blind man, for example, may learn something of the use of colour terms, but it can at the same time fairly be argued that he doesn't really know what they mean. But this is a different matter from the capacity of one person of sufficient age and endowed with the normal human faculties to understand the writing, speech or gestures of another even where they are not both members of a common culture. The procedure whereby, in Weber's examples, we come to understand what it is that the huntsman, the woodcutter and the ledger clerk are doing as distinguished from why they are doing it is intuitive only in the sense that our habitual understanding of our own language is intuitive. 'Linguistic competence', as that phrase has come to be used since the work of Chomsky, involves the successful application of rules which the language-user himself could not possibly state and is not conscious of following. But it is because the rules *are* followed by speaker and listener alike that effective communication is possible; and there is nothing mysterious about it except that linguistic research has not yet disclosed the exact 'deep structure' of the generative and transformational grammar which is common to all language-users whether they are aware of it or not. It doesn't arise in the sciences of nature, because language-learning is, with only limited and partial exceptions, peculiar to man. But this does not make it somehow immune to the methods of science.

There is, accordingly, no reason why the admittedly distinctive features of human actions, as opposed to natural events, should not

[120] *GAW*, p. 282 (Shils, pp. 179–80).
[121] It is true that Weber does sometimes use Dilthey's word '*nacherleben*'; but his own doctrine is still not Dilthey's, and at *GAW*, pp. 262–3 (Shils, p. 160) he expressly refers to *Nacherleben* as a term by which 'interpretation' in his own sense 'used to be called (although of course very incorrectly)'.

be fitted into the same common logical structure of idiographic explanation. This structure can be seen more clearly in the sort of example furnished by the equally historical but also much better grounded biological sciences. But it is not modified in the case of sociological explanation simply because human action is characteristically explained in terms of motives and reasons. Whatever may, in the end, turn out to be the nature of the neurophysiological or other laws underlying motives for actions, they can function just as effectively within the explanations which sociologists or historians put forward as do the contingently sufficient conditions cited by biological and, where appropriate, physical scientists. Nothing which I have said (or that Weber says himself) is inconsistent with Schutz's claim, made à propos of Weber, that 'The postulate of subjective interpretation has to be understood in the sense that all scientific explanations of the social world *can*, and for certain purposes *must*, refer to the subjective meaning of the actions of human beings from which social reality originates'.[122] Self-conscious human action is indeed what the social sciences are all about; but (as Schutz himself recognises) it lends itself to at least approximate and provisional generalisation without which it would be totally inexplicable – which it is not.

A typical example of the sort of idiographic explanation with which historians and sociologists are frequently concerned is a case where the problem consists in trying to discover what consideration was present in the mind of a designated agent as a result of which he adopted one alternative course of action rather than another. Weber gives as an example the respective strategies of Moltke and Benedek in the campaign of 1866. Given that we may safely assume that both generals were strongly motivated to win, we try to explain the course of the campaign in terms of the causes 'adequate' to account for the successive deviations of one or both of them from their 'ideal' strategies, whether these causes are false intelligence, misconception of the facts, faulty reasoning, personal temperament or considerations of some quite unstrategic kind.[123] The explanation which is duly offered rests in just the same way as an idiographic explanation in biological or physical science on the claim that a condition which could have been contingently sufficient to account for the puzzling difference from the implicit contrast case was in

[122] *Op. cit.* p. 62.
[123] *GAW*, p. 547 (Parsons, p. 111).

76

fact the decisive one, even though we cannot specify the conditions under which it would be bound to be so. The fact that the explanation is couched in terms of 'qualitatively heterogeneous' motives[124] means that it cannot be deduced from a law about motives in the way that explanations of the velocity of falling bodies can be deduced from Galileo's law. But provided that this heterogeneity is accurately reflected in a taxonomy which permits operational distinctions to be made, motives and reasons are as admissible as any of the countless theoretical terms whose referents are not directly observable but which nonetheless play a respectable empirical part in scientific explanations. Weber's position commits him neither to a belief in 'ghostly thrusts' nor to an acceptance of the Idealist thesis that the assignation of motives and reasons displaces, or even is incompatible with, causal explanation.

The form and nature of the laws which may one day be discovered behind our working truisms and approximate surmises about the determinants of action is a matter about which it is foolish to speculate in advance of empirical research. But it is only prudent to recognise that the terms in which our improved explanations will eventually be cast may be very remote from those to which we, no less than Weber, are still accustomed. To take a deliberately simple parallel, the notion of atmospheric pressure is at first sight very remote from the rough-and-ready generalisations about the boiling of water which served well enough for practical purposes for as long as those concerned did not stray too high above sea level. The upheavals brought about for common sense by twentieth-century developments in physical theory are more unexpected still; and it seems reasonable to suppose that with the progress of psychology similar upheavals are in store for our accustomed ways of describing what human beings think, say and do. It may well be, for example, that the language of motives will be preserved only in a metaphorical capacity, like the once literal language of 'humours', and that it will be replaced for scientific purposes, including those of the sociologist and the historian, by terms of a much more strictly behavioural, or indeed neurophysiological, kind. The terminology of Freud, although it has not been any better vindicated than Weber predicted by forming part of a well-confirmed general theory, still shows something of the way in which theoretical grounding might come to be furnished for

[124] *Ibid.*

77

provisional idiographic explanations couched in more common-sense terms; and it may be worth remembering that Freud himself sometimes, at least, regarded the terms which he coined as make-weights to be replaced in due course when the necessary discoveries in neurophysiology had been made. There are likewise some suggestive precedents for possible revisions of our customary vocabulary of human action in the results of recent studies of the behaviour of animals.[125] But the point is not to try to anticipate these changes. It is only to emphasise that our present lack of theoretical grounding for our idiographic explanations of human action is not to be taken as an *a priori* argument for the impossibility that it will be forthcoming – the error made in biology by the 'vitalists' until the issue was effectively decided against them by the findings of molecular biology. On the contrary: our acceptance of good idiographic explanations, when we can find them, presupposes that there is somewhere an adequate theoretical grounding for them. Weber's mistake did not lie in any failure to see that causal explanation of singular sequences of meaningful action is legitimate and practicable. It lay only in denying the dependence of such explanation on presumptive theoretical grounding at a different level.

[125] Weber was inclined to dismiss the relevance of animal studies to sociology on the grounds that 'we have no, or no reliable, means of establishing an animal's subjective state of mind' (*GAW*, p. 541 (Parsons, p. 104); cf. *GASS*, p. 461). But he goes on to acknowledge the results of studies of the survival function of social organisation in animals, and the possibility that further research might take the subject further than this.

Weber's – and Runciman's – mistake is to equate psychology with 'anatomy of the brain' studies!

VI

Thus far, my proposed corrections of Weber may seem to have been in one direction only. I have suggested that on the topics both of 'value-relevance' and of historical explanation he made not less but more concessions to the Idealists and the 'Historical School' than can be defended: so the question may well be asked, in what does the difference of kind between the natural and social sciences after all consist? It is true that the social sciences, even if cleansed of any lingering taint of Idealism, are very different from a science like classical mechanics. But then classical mechanics is not the model for natural science, and to show that the social sciences can never reach a sort of Laplacean consummation in which human actions in the remote future are as readily predictable as movements of the stars is not to show that explicability breaks down at the boundary between nature and culture. If, as I have been saying, Weber is still right to hold that there *is* a difference of kind between natural and social science, this difference must consist in something other than the fact that all the social, like many of the natural, sciences are at once unrestricted and open-ended. I have no intention in this essay of doing more than suggest in outline what sort of a difference it is. But I shall argue that this may best be seen by spelling out an account of the relation between explanation and description in the social sciences which Weber seems sometimes to hint at but never clearly to have perceived. This will serve not only to correct the third of Weber's errors which I listed at the beginning but at the same time to show how his doctrine of 'value-relevance', although untenable as it stands, derives from an implicit recognition of the single point at issue on which the Idealists rather than the Positivists are correct.

One way of putting it very generally would be to say that Weber recognised, with the Idealists, that the accounts which social scientists give of their chosen subject-matter are somehow discretionary, even after all the evidence is in, in a way that does not arise in the sciences of nature. Conceptual schemata may, of course, be said to be discretionary in natural science too: there is a sense in which we

79

are free, if we wish, to adhere to the Ptolemaic rather than the Copernican picture of the heavens, whatever may be the convenience of the Copernican. But however obstinately natural scientists of rival schools may cling to their chosen schemata, and however tortuous and haphazard the progress even of the most successful natural sciences may in fact have been, a consensus is arrived at in the end by reference to the relative ability of one set of concepts rather than another to furnish well-tested and wide-ranging theories. To be sure, this criterion operates in the social just as much as in the natural sciences. But in the social sciences, it is not in the same way a sole and sufficient criterion; only in the study of meaningful behaviour does the investigator feel the need to say, with Wittgenstein, that even where he is satisfied with his demonstration of causes and effects he still has a problem which is not causal but conceptual.[126]

A slightly different way of putting it might be to say that the study of meaningful behaviour raises problems of sense and reference in a way that the study of nature does not. In using this phrase, I am deliberately recalling the paper which Frege published in the *Zeitschrift für Philosophie und Philosophische Kritik* in 1892 under the title 'Über Sinn und Bedeutung' and which Weber could accordingly have read (although as far as I know he did not).[127] The numerous discussions to which it has led in recent English-speaking philosophy are for the most part concerned with topics in modal logic and the theory of meaning which fall quite outside of Weber's concerns. But the distinction which Frege drew between the *Sinn* of a term – the sense of the designation chosen – and its *Bedeutung*, or nominatum, does, I think, have a bearing on Weber's attempt to show why concept-formation in the social sciences poses the difficulties which it does. The distinction is closely related to Mill's distinction in the *System of Logic* (which Weber *had* read) between 'connotation' and 'denotation'.[128] But, as I have said, it is

---

126 *Op. cit.* II, xi: ' "The phenomenon is at first surprising, but a physiological explanation of it will certainly be found." Our problem is not a causal but a conceptual one.'

127 It is translated into English in both H. Feigl and W. Sellars, eds., *Readings in Philosophical Analysis* (New York, 1949) and Peter Geach and Max Black, eds., *Translations from the Philosophical Writings of Gottlob Frege* (Oxford, 1952).

128 See Book I, ch. II, sec. 5. Yet another possible source which might have led Weber to reflect on the distinction is Franz Brentano's *Psychologie von empirischen Standpunkt*, which had been published in 1874 and is

not the philosophical issues themselves which are relevant here so much as the particular significance for the sociologist, historian or anthropologist of the fact that terms whose referents are coextensive may differ radically in their *Sinn*. When he chooses – or, as Weber points out is often the case, coins – the terms by which he will designate and characterise a 'historical individual', he is not simply christening something by whatever is the handiest name, like Faraday adopting the suggestion of Whewell that the positive electric pole should be called the 'anode'. He may or may not, in any given case, be seeking to attach some evaluative overtone to it: although the terms of social science may not be 'value-relevant' in Weber's sense, it can still happen that, as I remarked in connection with the example of 'magic', they are used to signify the investigator's approval or condemnation. But the discretionary element in his conceptual scheme consists in more than a choice of names on the one hand and a decision to allow or disallow evaluative overtones on the other. It consists in the possibility of alternative *descriptions* of those areas of behaviour, and therefore those states of mind of designated agents, which he has chosen to study, irrespective of the validity (or otherwise) of the causally explanatory hypotheses which he is seeking to vindicate.

Let us go back to the construction of ideal types as Weber describes it. The process is, as Weber recognises, one in which the majority of historians engage without reflecting at all on its logic;[129] historians like himself who are self-consciously aware of their own procedures are relatively far between. But it is no criticism whatever of Weber's account that other practitioners may claim not to recognise their activity from it. Consciously or not, historians, sociologists and anthropologists do constantly make choices between alternative conceptual schemes for human thought and action, and they do so not solely by the test of whether one rather than another

known to have influenced Husserl. Husserl's own early work was known to Weber (and they were indeed colleagues on the editorial board of *Logos*); but it seems that despite occasional references to Husserl in the critique of Knies and a mention of his work, among that of several others, in the opening note to the essay of 1913 on *verstehende* sociology, Weber did not devote sustained attention to the doctrine of *Wesenschau*, presumably because of its avowed reliance on intuitions of 'essences' by the self-conscious subject.

129 See e.g. the opening paragraph of the 'Antikritisches Schlusswort zum "Geist der Kapitalismus"', *Archiv für Sozialwissenschaft und Sozialpolitik* XXXI (1910), reprinted in Baumgarten, *op. cit.* p. 172.

will in due course lead to, or be derivable from, a better-tested and more wide-ranging theory. Take the very first of Weber's examples which I cited: the ideal type of 'the Gothic'. For explanatory purposes, it functions, as we saw, in the same way as any idealisation in either a natural or a social science which can be usefully applied in the formulation of a prospective empirical generalisation or, better still, theory. Its justification resides in the sociologist's success in classifying apparently disparate works of art by reference to it and showing how the presence of 'Gothicness' of various degrees can be explained in terms of the influence of a designated set of psychological and/or sociological variables, ranging in this case, on Weber's view, from the discovery of the vault to the nuances of mediaeval theology. But this is not the only criterion by which the use of 'Gothic' in sociological or historical writing is decided; and it is this fact which distinguishes the role of idealisation in the social sciences, not (as Weber mistakenly claimed) the fact that ideal types are not employed at all by the sciences of nature. A sociologist's or historian's use of 'Gothic' may, and in practice often does, involve a decision to characterise the work of art (and therefore the meaningful behaviour of the artist) not, or not solely, as the product of those common causes by which other 'Gothic' works have likewise been produced, but as linked with them in terms of its meaning as explicitly distinguished from its cause. Such non-causal applications are not puns: describing both Chartres Cathedral and Mrs Radcliffe's *Mysteries of Udolpho* as 'Gothic' is not like describing both an artist wielding his pencil and a hangman disembowelling his victim as 'drawing'. Nor do they arise simply because 'Gothic' is, as it certainly is, a term not only 'open-textured' but also vague. They arise because of the manner in which any description of the meaning of a self-conscious human action carries with it a choice between alternative terms which differ not in *Bedeutung* but in *Sinn*.[130]

Consider again the example of 'magic'. To Weber its application to a designated social role in the relevant culture is, as we saw, a matter of 'value-relevance'. But, as I suggested, its application may

---

[130] Weber himself does use both these two terms. But the sense in which he does so is not only different from but much less precise than Frege's, even if Frege's critics are right to charge him, as they do, with imprecision in that he fails to give an adequate account of identity of *Sinn*.

remain discretionary even where it is used, as it often is, without any hint of evaluation whatever. If two sociologists are in dispute over whether a particular member of the culture which they are studying should or should not be described as a 'magician', they may be debating whether the ritual which it seems to be his role to enact follows from one rather than another set of necessary and contingently sufficient conditions. But they may equally be debating whether the ritual, however it is to be explained, is sufficiently close in terms of the attitude of its practitioners towards it to a ritual in a different culture which they have already agreed to call 'magical'; or whether the practitioners can properly be said, on the basis of what they say and do in the ritual, to be attempting to manipulate the unseen powers, which is one of the distinguishing marks of the magical as opposed either to the religious or to the purely pragmatic; or whether the practitioners' own insistence on describing the ritual as 'magical' should have priority over the observers' reluctance to do likewise. In these cases, the sociologist's difficulty is not one of science and/or logic in the customary sense any more than it is a difficulty about the intrusion of value-judgements. Yet it is the sort of difficulty which is characteristic of the formulation and use of 'ideal types' of meaningful behaviour.

How, then, do we decide which are the descriptive terms by which actions, or institutions, or cultures themselves ought to be designated? The idea that the agent's own description of his action – the one, that is, under which he would agree, once the range of alternatives has been suggested to him, that it most appropriately falls – raises among other difficulties that of the precise relations between intentions, motives and actions, which I have deliberately left to one side. But it can despite this be said with confidence both that there *is* a problem which Weber might have formulated correctly if only he had not been misled by his doctrine of 'value-relevance', and that the existence of it does vindicate his conviction that the methodology of concept-formation in the social sciences cannot be assimilated without remainder to that in the natural. Indeed, the almost exclusive preoccupation of philosophers of social science with problems in the logic of explanation has continued long after Weber to inhibit the recognition that the Idealists might, after all, be right about the alleged distinctiveness of the sciences of human action although wrong about the alleged distinctiveness of sociological explanation. It is a sensible philosophical maxim that when a protracted controversy seems incapable of settlement some assumption common to both sides should be abandoned. If I am right, the continuing and by now voluminous debate over the social sciences between the Positivists and the Idealists – which is nowadays to say, between the partisans of 'deductive-nomological' explanation on the one hand and 'rational' explanation on the other[131] – is a controversy of this kind; and a relatively small correction of Weber's view is enough to disclose one assumption, at least, which is wrongly shared by both contending parties.

There are two kinds of sociological writing in which the distinctive difficulty which confronts the social sciences is most clearly visible. The first is the cross-cultural comparison of ostensibly similar institutions, whether carried out by a comparative historian who himself stands outside of both or by a social anthropologist who approaches (as he can hardly help doing) the language and mores of an alien culture in terms of an implicit contrast with his own. The second is the kind of writing in which the historian or participant-observer is deliberately seeking not to explain to his readers why, or how, some feature of the culture which he is studying comes to be as it is but rather to convey to them what it is *like* in terms of the experience of those people who are or were members of that culture. Examples of both can be found in Weber's substantive writings. But they are only incidental to his principal purpose. His attempt to account for the emergence of Western industrial capitalism did lead him to contrast its institutions with those of cultures which might have, but did not, evolve in a similar direction, while his study of India, in particular, involved the attempt to elucidate the complex ethical and metaphysical beliefs of an alien culture in terms which the European reader brought up in a Christian tradition could sufficiently well grasp by reference to his own. But these considerations were subordinated throughout to the need to explain the difference in economic development between the two. Although, therefore, Weber does himself furnish examples which could be used to illustrate the point I wish to make, it may

---

131 See particularly Carl. G. Hempel, 'The Function of General Laws in History', first published in 1942 and reprinted in Patrick Gardiner, ed., *Theories of History* (Glencoe, Ill., 1959), pp. 344–56, for the first and William Dray, *Laws and Explanation in History* (Oxford, 1957), for the second; and for a more recent statement of their positions by the same two antagonists, their contributions to Sidney Hook, ed., *Philosophy and History* (New York, 1963).

once again be easier and less contentious if I ignore his own sociology and take my examples from elsewhere.

The best examples for the purpose are those afforded by the study of cultures wholly outside the traditions of the major civilisations of either the West or the East, such as the well-known accounts given by Evans-Pritchard of the beliefs and mores of the Azande and Nuer of the Southern Sudan.[132] Evans-Pritchard's work has, as it happens, attracted considerable attention from philosophers as well as anthropologists concerned with the problems raised by the interpretation of alien and indeed puzzling systems of belief which are nevertheless internally coherent and strongly held. Much of this discussion, however, has revolved round the notion of 'rationality' and its application in cross-cultural contexts, and I prefer to bypass this for the same reason that I have ignored Weber's own discussion of 'rationality' and its forms. For my purpose here, the usefulness of studies such as Evans-Pritchard's is that they illustrate and confirm both Weber's argument that what is at once subjective and culturally unique is still scientifically explicable in principle and his simultaneous concession to the Idealist view that such things cannot be described simply by reference to the terms of a relevant set of established general laws but require the framing of qualitative distinctions deriving from their apparent meaning to the subjects themselves.

The anthropologist's explanations – if he is concerned to offer any, which he need not be – may be of many different kinds. But where the purpose of his account, whether overt or latent, is explanatory, the observer's categories have priority over the subjects'. He must, of course, identify his chosen explananda correctly. He must know the language properly, he must be able to tell whether his informants are joking or otherwise misleading him, and he must be confident of discriminating between expressions of literal belief and purely symbolic expressions of emotion. But if, at the end of the exercise, he decides to categorise, say, what the Nuer have said to him about Kwoth, the Spirit of the Above, as 'religious' belief, it does not matter that this invokes a distinction which may be entirely alien and even unacceptable to the Nuer themselves. Its legitimacy rests on the testable empirical generalisations which he can frame, or hopes to be able to frame, in terms of it and its

---

[132] See E. E. Evans-Pritchard, *Witchcraft, Oracles and Magic among the Azande* (Oxford, 1937); and *Nuer Religion* (Oxford, 1956).

potential convenience in isolating a dependent variable which can be causally linked to independent variables of other kinds.

When, however, the observer wishes not so much to explain to his readers why the culture he has studied is as it is in some designated aspect, or simply to report to them certain empirical facts about it which he thinks will be of interest to them, as to transmit to his readers a sense of what living in that culture is like, he has obviously to give the culture's own conceptual categories at least an initial priority. He will no doubt have to supplement and amplify them with his own; but he will be doing so in order to clarify rather than dispute them. It is a commonplace of sociology that if people think things are real then the observer, too, must treat them as real, however much better he may think he knows the facts of the matter than they. But this way of putting it conceals rather than illuminates the difference between the observer's need to acknowledge his subjects' definition of their situation, even if they are wrong, for the purpose of description and his need to be willing where necessary to reject it altogether for the purpose of explanation. Only to the degree that mis*description* is at issue is it a relevant charge against an account of human institutions and behaviour that it is ethnocentric, or unhistorical, or unsubtle, or imperceptive, or patronising, or any of an extensive range of similar characterisations familiar from reviews and criticisms of works of ethnography, narrative history, journalism or indeed realistic (or would-be realistic) fiction. Such a charge is not a charge of inaccuracy, for the account in question may contain no statement which is untrue. It is rather a charge of having either ignored or overridden the subjects' categories and priorities where it can be shown to be inappropriate to do so.

Now to cite such criticisms as being relevant to sociological but not to natural-scientific writing may seem inconsistent with my repeated defence of Weber against the charge of intuitionism: for if these are the criteria which *verstehende* sociology has to satisfy, it may appear after all to involve the 'reliving' of the experience of the subjects in question in some sort of inaccessible Diltheyan way. But although it is true that sociological description raises difficulties over and above those of sociological explanation, it does not follow that the door has been reopened to the intuitionists. This is so for two connected reasons. The first is that even for the avowed purpose of grasping and conveying the 'feel', or the 'flavour' or the 'spirit' of a social situation or an institution, as opposed to that of merely reporting the facts of it, it remains true that no more esoteric cognitive capacity is required of either the observer or his readers than that of coming to understand the meaning and use of the relevant terms. The second is that the technique by which this is typically best done is not a sort of prolonged contemplation out of which a flash of autistic empathy is suddenly generated but by suggesting and defending equivalences of meaning in a contrasted culture. If someone chooses still to say that we can never be completely certain that we have correctly understood the words and deeds of the members of the culture we are studying, the answer is that this is indeed so; but there is no more that can be done about it,[133] and this, so far from vindicating the need for some faculty of understanding peculiar to human behaviour, serves merely to confirm that there is no such thing. Just as all practising social scientists are Idealists in the innocuous sense that they recognise that human behaviour does have a meaning to its agents, so they are all Behaviourists in the innocuous sense that they recognise that only observable behaviour (or records of observation of it) can be studied in the first place.

Let me go back to Evans-Pritchard's accounts of Nuer and Zande culture. As before, I am not concerned whether his accounts are entirely correct or how far a more recent observer who had the benefit of subsequent advances in ethnographic theory or methods might wish to qualify them, but only with the illustration which they provide of the distinctive problems of social science. Evans-Pritchard is not, as it happens, concerned to more than a limited degree with the explanation of the beliefs and practices of the peoples studied. Not only is there very little evidence on which an explanation might be based, but he is himself thoroughly dismissive of would-be theories such as Frazer's or Durkheim's which seek to fit all magic and/or religion to some one common paradigm. He

---

[133] Positivists' scepticism along these lines is admittedly more compelling than Idealists' scepticism of the possibility of historical knowledge: see particularly W. V. Quine, *Word and Object* (Cambridge, Mass., 1960), ch. 2, where the problems of learning an alien language are linked to the difficulties inherent in the notion of synonymy. But it is equally immaterial to the practising sociologist, anthropologist or historian, who can only proceed on the assumption that he will be able to make the necessary discriminations and identifications as well in the alien language as in his own.

does not, however, any more than Weber, conclude from this that particular designated features of a system of beliefs and practices cannot therefore be accounted for in principle, and the conclusions which he puts forward can readily be analysed under the three separate headings of first, identification; second, explanation; and third, description.

To identify the beliefs and practices of the Azande and Nuer requires first and most obviously a mastery of the language, and once we accept this, *pace* Quine, as feasible we may accept Evans-Pritchard as capable of distinguishing the content of the words and gestures of the Zande and Nuer as well as they can themselves, even if he is no better able than they are to set out the latent rules which underlie it. This is not to suggest that this is easy to do. Apart from the technical difficulties of the language itself, he may conclude (and at several points does) that his informants are themselves confused and their beliefs or attitudes ambiguous.[134] But he can in principle report their beliefs and practices in a way that is equally accessible to any other trained observer. In practice, trained observers may well differ over such questions as whether a Zande does literally believe that his neighbour is a witch or a Nuer that migratory birds are visiting God's country when they leave Nuerland. But this is no reason to regard these as other than questions of fact, and Evans-Pritchard's own evidence suggests strongly that the answer to the first is yes and to the second no: whatever Durk-

---

[134] It is, of course, true that the languages of some cultures may be seriously impoverished relative to the languages of others. But this is not the same sort of problem as my earlier example of the blind man lacking the capacity to come to understand the meaning of colour terms: see e.g. John R. Searle, *Speech Acts* (Cambridge, 1969), pp. 19–20, for a concise statement of the principle that a language is always capable of prospective enrichment to accommodate novel meanings. Weber, although he did not doubt the ability of the trained historian to understand the alien cultures of the past, was uncharacteristically sceptical of the ability of the trained ethnographer to understand the behaviour of 'primitives' (*Naturmenschen*) any better than that of animals: see *GAW*, p. 541 (Parsons, p. 104 and note 27 where Parsons rightly remarks that 'It can be said with considerable confidence that a competently trained anthropological fieldworker is in a position to obtain a level of insight into the states of mind of a people whom he has carefully studied which is quite comparable, if not superior, to that of the historian of a civilisation at all widely different from his own'). Cf. also *GAW*, p. 259 (Shils, p. 157). On the other hand, he willingly recognised that in 'civilised' society men are no more knowledgeable about the facts of their economic and social life than in societies we call primitive: see *GAW*, p. 473, cf. p. 577 (G & M, p. 139).

heimians might suppose, the Azande do literally believe in witch-craft just as much as we believe in medicine, and whatever Frazerians might suppose, the Nuer are as well aware as ourselves of using metaphor and fantasy in much of what they have to say. There is always the possibility of error in seeking to ascertain what someone believes, or what are his intentions in performing a ritual, or what he holds to be morally or aesthetically good or bad. But it is not something which is at the observer's discretion, however different the language and culture which he is studying may be from his own.

This is equally so when the observer moves on from identifying and reporting to categorising and explaining the behaviour he has observed. The classifications which the observer adopts, the generalisations which he holds valid and the hypotheses which he seeks to test are all governed by the intersubjective criteria of public testability common to natural and social science alike. It is by these criteria that Evans-Pritchard both rejects Durkheim's and Frazer's attempts at general theories and advances limited causal hypotheses of his own. As in all cases where meaningful behaviour is being studied, there is the difficulty in deciding at what point identification breaks off and explanation properly begins. For example, one of several features of the dances of Zande witch-doctors by which the observer may be puzzled is the exaggeration of their move-ments; and the answer lies, as might readily be expected, in the symbolic meaning to which the dancers seek to give expression. This, therefore, is evidently an instance of Weber's 'direct' as opposed to 'explanatory' understanding. But it quickly shades over into a request for explanation in a manifestly causal sense, whether the observer's interest is idiographic – say, in the question why a particular spectator is the target of the symbolic witch-hunt – or nomothetic – say, in the relations of scapegoating to social and psychological stress. The observer may find his enquiry blocked at any of these stages. Evans-Pritchard reports that the symbolism of the dances may be misunderstood even by the audience, and that the witch-doctor is sometimes merely trying to show off or to retain a particular spectator's attention. The story of a particular case of witchcraft and its detection may be too complex to unravel even with a thorough general knowledge of the ideology and mechanism of witch-hunting as a technique of social control. Psychological theories of witch-hunting behaviour are notoriously difficult to test empirically even if they are more modestly and circumspectly framed than they are usually apt to be. Even explanation by reference to alien influence is likely to be difficult to establish conclusively, and itself presupposes some psychological or sociological generalisation about the acceptability of some but not other doctrines or practices: Evans-Pritchard gives evidence, for example, of Dinka influence on the Nuer based on the timing and geography of divergences from standard Nuer custom, but he is very wary of inferring too much from correlations of this kind. Yet in all these examples and any others like them, there is no difficulty in recognising the procedures of normal scientific method. The ethnographic observer, however strong his wish to challenge the hypotheses of his colleagues and however different from theirs his particular interest in the culture in question, is still doing science and not philosophy. His explanations may be mistaken and incomplete, but they are not 'subjective' in any sense which does not equally apply to the field geologist's account of the head waters of the Upper Towy.

It is another matter, however, when it comes to what Evans-Pritchard himself speaks of as 'an understanding of the fundamental character' of Nuer religion, or what he calls the question of 'what may be said to be that which is expressed in the social and cultural forms we have been studying', or his contention that it is 'an oversimplification and a misunderstanding' to say, as another observer has done, that Nuer religion is 'a religion of fear'.[135] These are questions which can hardly be said to be outside of the ethnographer's proper academic concerns. Yet they are not questions which further empirical evidence is likely to settle; and no more are they to be settled by mere convention. A dispute over whether to call Nuer religion a 'religion of fear' is not just a dispute as to whether a treelike bush should be called a bush or a tree, or even whether a substance which satisfies all the chemical tests for gold but emits a new sort of radiation should be called 'gold'.[136] Rival ethnographers who agree in their observations of Nuer speech and behaviour but dispute the appositeness of each other's descriptions of it are disagreeing over the implications of the precedent which will be set by accepting one form of account in preference to

---

[135] These quotations are all taken from the concluding chapter of *Nuer Religion*.

[136] This example is borrowed directly from Waissmann's remarks about 'open texture' (*op. cit.* p. 120).

another. In the celebrated phrase of Wittgenstein, they are arguing over 'forms of life': but since this phrase is by no means unambiguous in its turn,[137] it may be safer to say no more than that since there cannot be a meaning-neutral language in which to talk about meaning in the way that logic furnishes a topic-neutral language in which to talk about validity, the ethnographer's task can never be straightforwardly or exclusively an empirical one. A more extreme and even paradoxical way of putting it is Lévi-Strauss's remark that the ethnographer's analysis of myth is itself a myth[138] – a statement which seems wilfully to obscure the possibility that a structural analysis of Lévi-Strauss's kind might furnish at least a part of the answer to the causal questions about the origin, transmission and perpetuation of the myths he describes. But the fact that serious ethnographers say such things at all is itself illuminating. Evans-Pritchard's account of the Azande and Nuer could hardly be more matter-of-fact. But even he suggests at the very end of *Nuer Religion* that there comes a point in the attempt to describe the religious experience of Nuer at which the anthropologist must give way to the theologian.

All this may seem to have taken us some distance from Weber's concerns. But despite his rather cavalier attitude to the study of primitive peoples, Weber does in fact touch on these same issues, although from a different standpoint, in his critique of Eduard Meyer. His principal criticism of Meyer is that Meyer fails to recognise that the historian's interests are not dictated solely by a concern with the events which have been 'historically effective' in their influence on the present day. He doesn't of course suggest that historians ought not to analyse 'objective possibilities', as Meyer had done in attributing to the Battle of Marathon the decisive influence which made possible the emergence of a free-thinking Hellenic culture whose ideas we have ourselves inherited in the place of the closed, theocratic culture which would have evolved under a Persian protectorate. But he insists that causal explanation, here as always, 'grasps only part of the matter'. Thus

---

[137] Perhaps less obscure than Wittgenstein's dicta about forms of life is his remark that 'perspicuous representation' (*übersichtliche Darstellung*) 'produces just that understanding which consists in "seeing connections" . . .it designates the form of account we give, the way we look at things. (Is this a "Weltanschauung"?)' (*op. cit.* para. 122).

[138] Claude Lévi-Strauss, *Mythologiques I: Le Cru et le Cuit* (Paris, 1964), p. 20.

when the historian considers Marx's *Capital* as a 'historical individual' and chooses how to characterise it for his purposes, he will
have regard not only to the question 'from what materials Marx
constructed his work and how the genesis of his ideas was historically conditioned' but to the question of its 'unique intellectual
content', and he will conceive of this by reference not to its physical
properties as print and paper or even its membership of some
designated class of 'literary product' but to its 'meaning' in an
explicitly non-causal sense.[139] It is this, indeed, which justifies the
assertion that history is in some sense art[140] – a remark in which
Weber seems to be echoing an earlier remark in the editorial of
1904 that all descriptions 'bear the mark of artistic representation'.[141]

Weber here comes very close to recognising that the special
conceptual problems of the social sciences are problems not of
explanation but of description. But the trouble, of course, is that
the solution of his own with which he seeks to put right Meyer's
mistake is a solution in terms of his (or Rickert's) conception of
'value-relevance'. This has two unfortunate results. First, it under-
mines his otherwise sensible remarks about the use of ideal types
in formulating the 'series of abstractions' by reference to which the
historian's hypotheses are framed. Second, it depicts the 'artistic'
aspect of historical or sociological description as a sort of imposi-
tion of the standards of the observer's own culture, when it is in
fact perfectly possible – as the example of Evans-Pritchard well
shows – for him deliberately to subordinate his '*Kulturwertideen*'
to those of the subjects whom he is studying. Yet Weber's concessions to the Idealists, even as expressed in the editorial of 1904, all
derive from his awareness that behind every explanation of social
behaviour, however well validated the reports on which it rests and
the causal connections between operationally defined variables
which it establishes, there lurks an option to accept or reject the
overtones of meaning implicit in the conceptual schema within
which it is framed. Seen in this way, Weber's preoccupation with
the 'transitoriness' of ideal types is no longer at odds with his
simultaneous insistence on the universality of cause and effect. It
might still be objected that the ideal types of natural science are

139 *GAW*, pp. 251, 253 (Shils, pp. 149, 151).
140 *GAW*, p. 247 (Shils, p. 145).
141 *GAW*, p. 209 (Shils, p. 107).

transitory, too: as I have already remarked, biology furnishes a more instructive paradigm against which to match sociology than mechanics does, and the history of natural science is full of dilemmas of choice between rival conceptual schemes. But the reformulation of ideal types which biological science requires does not involve a problem of meanings in the way that reformulation of ideal types of beliefs, values, art forms and the rest involves a problem of meanings. These are the very things which distinguish the sociological evolution of cultures from the biological evolution of species, and although cultures can, no less than species, be objects of authentic scientific enquiry, for the purpose of description they need not, and often should not, be characterised by reference only to the terms which are most useful for the purpose of identifying, reporting, classifying and as far as possible explaining the behaviour of their members. Put in this sort of way, therefore, and shorn of the doctrine of 'value-relevance', Weber's remarks about the importance of the 'guiding point of view' to the sociologist's construction of his conceptual scheme[142] can be read in a sense which justifies his conviction that despite the unity of science there *are* conceptual problems in the sciences of human behaviour of a kind from which the sciences of nature are spared.

Now this contrast between identifying, reporting, classifying and explaining on the one hand and describing on the other might be argued to be not merely an imprecise but an idiosyncratic use of 'describe'. But although not the only, or to philosophers even the commonest, use of the term it is a perfectly familiar one; and although its boundaries are admittedly unclear, this may help to show why Weber failed to recognise that the problem he was seeking to solve falls neither under the heading of explanation on the one hand nor of evaluation on the other.[143] Seen like this, the problem of description, like the problem of idealisation, can be looked at equally well in terms of descriptive propositions or descriptive terms. Descriptive propositions can, like any propositions, have a truth-value, which terms in themselves can not. But it is not the truth-value of a descriptive proposition which determines its merits

[142] *GAW*, p. 184 (Shils, p. 84).
[143] I have tried to explore the distinction a little more fully in a paper under the title 'Describing' (*Mind*, forthcoming), which was in turn prompted by S. E. Toulmin and K. Baier, 'On Describing', *Mind* n.s. LXI (1952), 13–38.

as a description except to the extent that the historian's, socio-logist's or anthropologist's description is disqualified if it asserts to be true something which is in fact false. The success of a description of a culture or an institution or of the values and beliefs of its members depends on its success in performing not an artistic so much as a pictorial function. The terms which the sociologist chooses must first of all serve adequately the referential function which is a prerequisite of reportage and explanation; but they must in addition be *apposite*, just as the connected series of reports which constitute his descriptions must be not merely accurate but apposite too. It is in general much easier to say when a descriptive term, or a description itself, is not apposite than when it is. But it is in principle apposite to the degree that it would enable the qualified but unbiassed participant to recognise the chosen aspects of the culture or institution in the description given.

I have said already that sociological description, in the sense in which I am using the term, characteristically proceeds by the sug-gestion and defence of equivalences of meaning in a contrasted culture. Equivalence of meaning is itself a complex and often controversial matter, and there are in any case no clear dividing-lines between either explanation and description on the one hand or description and evaluation on the other. But there is no lack of sociological writing in which a descriptive purpose can readily be distinguished from an explanatory, if only by the use of such phrases as 'it was as though . . .', or 'in something of the same way . . .', or 'it would have seemed to an earlier generation that...' in contrast to 'therefore', 'because', or 'as a result'. Suggested equivalences of meaning in these contexts may be quite specific, as when an ethnographer suggests that talk of demonic possession and exorcism in a so-called primitive culture can be equated with talk of virus infection and immunology in our own. More often, they proceed by metaphor or analogy, as when, say, a political belief is described as 'as it were, a religion', or the attitudes of twentieth-century liberals to the accommodating Negro are equated with those of nineteenth-century liberals to the deserving poor, or adjectives like 'Whiggish' or 'Bismarckian' or 'baroque' or 'rabbinical' are deliberately transposed from their proper temporal or cultural context into another one. Sometimes, they may almost be flippant, as when a historian likens going on a mediaeval pilgrim-age to going on a twentieth-century Caribbean cruise, or an ethnographer describes the taboos and rituals of a highly developed industrial culture in the terms commonly reserved for those of *Naturmenschen*. But the serious academic purpose which all these rhetorical devices are being employed to serve is that of illuminating the social context in which the actions of the subjects in question were performed, the nature of the psychological and institutional assumptions which informed their attitudes, motives and desires, and the significance, both overt and symbolic, which their roles and activities had to themselves. It is true that this does not go on in isolation from the explanatory criteria by which the subjects' behaviour is classified: there underlies all these parallels of meaning the assumption that (*ceteris paribus*) common causes yield common effects. But analogies such as those I have cited are not vindicated by subsuming the behaviour being compared under a common theory but by defending the similarity of meaning by reference to some common category of thought and feeling. Even if there is not quite the contrast to be drawn between explaining and understanding which Jaspers, in particular, maintained,[144] there is still a contrast to be drawn between answering the question why people have done what they have done and describing (or even 'depicting') what it meant to them.

As Weber's own choices testify, the history of art affords some of the most effective examples. In the critique of Meyer, he draws an explicit contrast between merely 'philological' interpretation of the meaning of a work of art or literature, which is no more than a preliminary task of the historian, and 'interpretative' analysis in terms of possible value-relevance which 'sets out "problems" for the causal work of history'.[145] It is still not the right contrast, for reasons which I hope by now I need not repeat. But some of what Weber says in terms of it comes quite close to the distinction drawn later, and with rather more success, by Panofsky between 'iconographical' and 'iconological' analysis of meaning.[146] 'Iconographical' meaning, like Weber's 'philological' meaning, is simply a matter of knowing the language: the Renaissance art historian can hardly

---

[144] Weber acknowledges a debt to Jaspers, and in particular his *Allgemeine Psychopathologie*, both in an introductory note to the paper on *verstehende* sociology (*GAW*, p. 427 n1) and the opening remarks of *Economy and Society* (*GAW*, p. 527 (Parsons, pp. 87–8)).

[145] *GAW*, p. 262 (Shils, p. 160).

[146] Erwin Panofsky, *Studies in Iconology: Humanistic Themes in the Art of the Renaissance* (New York, 1939), pp. 3–31.

start without knowing that a male figure with a knife represents St Bartholomew and a female figure holding a peach is a personification of truthfulness, whereas an Australian bushman, as Panofsky puts it himself, 'would be unable to recognise the subject of a Last Supper; to him it would only convey the idea of an excited dinner party'.[147] 'Iconological' meaning, on the other hand, is a matter of understanding the Last Supper 'as a document of Leonardo's personality, or of the civilisation of the Italian High Renaissance, or of a peculiar religious attitude' – an account which parallels much of what Weber says à propos of the example of Goethe's letters to Frau von Stein. There is still the same implicit concern with causal connection: if the historian's interest is directed to Leonardo's or Goethe's unconscious motives he is likely to be seeking direct links between psychological, not to say pathological, variables; and even where he is concerned with describing it in terms of its iconological relation to the culture of its period, he will assume that the common meanings to which otherwise very different works of art may be said to give expression spring from common influences acting upon the artists who fashioned them. But his curiosity will still be unsatisfied, and his task therefore incomplete, even if he has what is, to him, a sufficiently convincing hypothesis to meet every one of the explanatory questions which have puzzled him. The Idealists' dissatisfaction with the Positivist account of explanation is misplaced only because it is not *explanation* which is at issue. The Positivist account does indeed fail to reflect an important part of what art historians or 'cultural scientists' in general are actually trying to do. But the fact which it glosses over (or in many Positivist writings simply ignores) is not that explanation of a different sort is being practised in the sciences of culture but that something is being practised which cannot be subsumed under that heading at all.

To those of Weber's commentators who adhere at least implicitly to an exclusive distinction between 'facts' and 'values' all this is merely an argument for saying that the social sciences are 'value-relevant' after all, or even that they are permeated, and bound to be so, by value judgements in a still stronger sense.[148] But to draw this

---

[147] *Ibid.* p. 11.
[148] This is, for example, the position of one of Weber's fiercest critics, Leo Strauss, who seeks to argue in his *What is Political Philosophy? and Other Studies* (Glencoe, Ill., 1959) that 'Generally speaking, it is im-

conclusion is to ignore the distinction which Weber clearly recognised, even if he failed to take it far enough, between understanding the 'value-ideas' of a given culture and either accepting or rejecting them oneself. Historians and sociologists may seek to describe, as well as merely to report and if possible explain, the moral, aesthetic and political values of their chosen subjects, and when they do so they will employ theoretical terms whose meaning reflects it. We can accordingly say, if we will, that in bringing out the distinctions which he wishes to stress in his account of human action the observer 'enters the domain of morality'.[149] But this assertion is false if that phrase is taken to entail that the observer himself has to make a moral judgement one way or the other about the agents whom he has observed. No doubt, the distinction between description and evaluation is often obscured in practice. Many art historians overtly assume the role not merely of expositor but of critic,[150] just as many economists and political scientists quite deliberately (as I have already remarked) flout Weber's injunctions against using the lecture-room as a party rostrum, and the point at which exposition slides over into advocacy is not always easy to discern. But this doesn't constitute a counter-argument to my claim that description, as I have used that term, can be distinguished not only from reportage and explanation on one side but from evaluation on the other; that it is this, and not the problem of 'values', which poses difficulties for the social scientist from which the natural scientist is spared; and that by drawing this distinction it is possible to endorse Weber's view that concept-formation in social science is somehow discretionary without being committed to the further concessions which he mistakenly made to the Idealists' side.

I have no intention of trying explicitly to frame the criteria by which the success of sociological description as opposed to explana-

possible to understand thought or action or work without evaluating it' (p. 21).

[149] This way of putting it is taken from Hampshire, *op. cit.* p. 168.

[150] Cf. Weber's discussion of the use of the term 'progress' in the social sciences, which, as he says, may be used in either an evaluative sense or in either one of two non-evaluative senses – first, increasing differentiation, and second, improved success in applying technical means to specified ends. The example which he cites (from Robert Liefmann) is that of the 'economically correct' action of producers who destroy goods to create a shortage and thus raise prices above costs: this may be 'technical progress', but it does not follow that it *ought* to be done. See *GAW*, pp. 511–14 (Shils, pp. 34–6).

tion should be assessed. This is a task for philosophy, and I am not a philosopher either by training or profession, any more than Weber was. But it is a symptom of the difference between the sciences of man and of nature that the practising sociologist finds himself confronted with philosophical questions whether he likes it or not. On the Positivist view, the task of philosophy in social as in natural science is limited to the logical elucidation of accepted practice, and the philosopher can contribute nothing to the advancement of research until research has yielded discoveries sufficiently deserving to be elucidated. But this view dismisses *a priori* not only much of what sociologists, anthropologists and historians do but also many of the sources of a non-'scientific' kind which they find illuminating. This apparent illumination may, of course, be spurious. The practising sociologist who thinks his conceptualisation of human action has been improved by a reading of Wittgenstein[151] or Tolstoy may simply be mistaken: or at least, he may be mistaken except to the extent that philosophy and literature may furnish suggestions of explanatory hypotheses which scientific investigation subsequently confirms. But for myself, at least, I have to say that neither as a practising sociologist nor as a human agent do I find this plausible. I am constantly puzzled by questions of meaning as opposed to cause and of appositeness as opposed to validity, and my persistent awareness of descriptive discretion in the practice of sociological research is not to be appeased by mere dismissal out of hand. The usefulness of Weber's *Wissenschaftslehre* is that it not only acknowledges but seeks to analyse and justify this awareness; and the usefulness of this section of my critique of him is, I hope, that it suggests a way of doing so which avoids the pitfalls into which Weber himself was drawn by his ingenious but mistaken conjunction of 'value-relevance', 'understanding' and 'ideal types'.

[151] I expect to be reminded that Wittgenstein himself insisted that philosophy 'leaves the world as it is' (*op. cit.* para. 124 and elsewhere). But to this the rejoinder has rightly been made by his commentators: 'Yes, except for concepts.'

VII

I said in the opening paragraph of this essay that if my attempted correction of Weber's arguments, as I read them, is well-founded, this will constitute at least some modest contribution to the philosophy of social science. The reader will by now have judged for himself how far this claim has been sustained. But it may still be worthwhile for me to offer in conclusion a slightly fuller statement of the reasons for my belief that Weber deserves this degree of attention. On my own account, after all, his methodological writings are not only dated, fragmentary and unsystematic, but mistaken on three significant counts. Is it not, therefore, possible that the relative neglect of them in the English-speaking world may after all be quite justified?

It is true that some of the increasing interest which now attaches to Weber's writings on methodology is historical rather than philosophical. He was not a philosopher of social science in the sense of, say, Mill before him or Popper after, and his initial attempt to compromise between the rival dogmas of the 'Classical' and 'Historical' schools can be read more plausibly as the reflection of a practising economic historian's need to clear his mind than as an intended contribution to the running debate between Positivism and Idealism. It is not irrelevant to recall that his methodological writings began with a critique of two economists and a statement of editorial policy for a social science journal, and that two of the later essays are no more than extended book reviews. Yet if one contrasts Weber with Mill, there is a sense in which his interests were more philosophical as well as less. Mill was, no doubt, a philosopher as well as a political economist on any definition: his methodology of the social sciences forms part of a treatise not of political economy but of logic, and he was palpably better versed than Weber in the problems of sense and reference, induction and probability, and the relation of empirical generalisations to causal laws. Yet it could, in a way, be said of Mill that for him the problems of the social sciences were not *philosophical* problems at all so much as technical ones. Induction is difficult, controlled experimentation is impossible, and sociologists are all too prone, as Mill said of Comte himself, to substitute purely promissory manifestoes for empirical confirmation of their pretended laws. But Mill had less doubts about what needed to be done than about how it might be feasible to do it. Weber's concern with the recurring discretion which the sociologist has to exercise in framing his concepts finds no expression in Mill's 'Logic of the Moral Sciences'. Mill may have understood better than Weber the logic of the distinction between sense and reference; but he never saw the distinction as raising a peculiar difficulty for the investigator of self-conscious human action as opposed to the investigator of nature. Weber, by contrast, although he acknowledged the validity of the Positivists' arguments, including many of Mill's own, at the same time acknowledged that there is a serious case on the other side. For all his dismissal of 'Hegelian Emanatism', he did not regard the whole Idealist tradition, as some of the most distinguished English philosophers of the twentieth century have done, as a succession of inflated muddles too obviously mistaken, if not merely vacuous, to be taken seriously. He did not seek to deny that Dilthey, Rickert and the rest had pointed to the existence of some distinctive characteristic which the sciences of nature do not share with the sciences of man; he sought only to show that this recognition must not be conceded at the price of denying what the Positivists are perfectly right to affirm.

The English-speaking reader, who comes to Weber's methodology from the tradition of Mill, cannot fail to be struck by how much twentieth-century discussion by philosophers writing in English was anticipated by Weber. It is not simply that his concern with the role of laws in historical explanation, the relation of motives to actions, and the difference between the attribution of reasons and of causes has since been taken up as widely as it has: these themes, after all, had been the concern of methodologists of the social sciences ever since the eighteenth century and were likely to remain so. But Weber expounded methodological individualism long before Popper, prescriptivism long before Hare and the significance of the notion of 'following a rule' long before Wittgenstein. Admittedly, neither catholicity of interests nor skill (or luck) in anticipation of later intellectual fashions are in themselves an authentication of excellence. But the moral to which Weber's eclecticism points, and which the subsequent history of the philosophy of social science has served amply to confirm, is that a successful account of the logic of social scientific method requires the occupation and defence of a selected area of the middle ground against the extremists of both contending parties. It occasionally happens in a long-standing dispute of this kind that one side turns out to be wholly right and the other wholly wrong: in the present century, the example of Bergson is particularly sobering. But once the simple-minded distinction between 'fact' and 'value' as exhaustive alternatives has been recognised as such, it becomes possible still to vindicate the dissatisfaction of the Idealists without falling into the errors which have brought their own positive doctrines into such disrepute.

This dissatisfaction, moreover, is bound to be the more convincing when it comes from a practitioner of whom it has been said that he is not merely the greatest of sociologists, but *the* sociologist (and, indeed, that this opinion 'is affirmed today by the majority of sociologists the world over').[152] Those of Weber's commentators who either ignore his methodology altogether, or treat it as an almost irrelevant adjunct to the main body of his work,[153] have done him no less of a disservice than those who have claimed his authority for a methodology which his own substantive writings disconfirm.[154] Consistency between precept and practice is not, of course, enough to vindicate the precept; however successful Weber's practice, his precepts remain in need of substantial correction. But the success of his practice, and perhaps still more its range, qualify him better than any sociologist, anthropologist, or historian of this century to select and define the controversies which require to be resolved if we are ever to have an account of the social sciences which is at the same time philosophically defensible and also consistent with the actual achievements (few though these may yet be) of those engaged in them. It is intriguing, although fruitless, to speculate what might have been the influence of a systematic and full-length treatise on methodology by Weber if he had ever carried out his rather half-hearted promises to write one. Only the introductory sections of *Economy and Society* can be claimed as at all a

152 Aron, *op. cit.* II, 245.
153 The best-known commentary on Weber in English, Reinhard Bendix's *Max Weber: an Intellectual Portrait* (London, 1960) is particularly disappointing from this standpoint: as justly remarked by Fleischmann (*op. cit.* p. 190 n1), it fails to live up to the promise of its title.
154 The most influential culprit in this category is Parsons.

definitive statement, and even these are less closely, or at least less obviously, related to his substantive researches than might be wished. But there can be no doubt at all of Weber's consistent and almost obsessive awareness, from the time of his breakdown up to his death, of the questions which a systematic treatise would have to answer. He was not, as we have seen, concerned that the answers might not fit the preconceptions of practitioners who had never in fact reflected on the assumptions underlying their chosen procedures of research. But he was concerned that a methodology adequate for the industrial psychologist should be no less adequate for the historian of Renaissance art. I remarked in an earlier section on the tendency for discussions of the philosophy of the social sciences to be dominated by examples carefully chosen to the intended advantage of either the Positivist or the Idealist side; and it is only to be expected that specialists will regard their own particular branch of the sciences of man as the paradigm against which any suggested methodology should first be tested. But to someone such as Weber, whose studies extended from the ethic of Confucianism to the German stock exchange and from the determinants of variation in workers' productivity to the early history of Western music, this could hardly become a danger. His philosophy of social science might be mistaken, but it would never be either parochial or philistine.

Readers well versed in the intellectual history of Weber's period may still wish to argue that his mistakes are no more instructive than those of his less ecumenical contemporaries. If it is something of an accident that the interest of his methodological writings should not have been acknowledged sooner, it is no less an accident that they should now be so much better known than those of, say, Simmel, who foresaw with a melancholy prescience that his posthumous influence would be so quickly and so widely diffused as never to be properly recognised.[155] If there is any one particular reason, it is perhaps the continuance of the debate about 'values'; and this carries the double irony that Weber, while rejecting the principal arguments on which it feeds, at the same time helped to protract it by expounding under the heading of 'value-relevance' an argument which should have nothing to do with 'values' at all. But the history of ideas is rich in ironies of this kind. An explanation of Weber's influence can no doubt be convincingly advanced which relates it

[155] See his 'Nachgelassenes Tagebuch', *Logos* VII (1919), 121.

both to the circumstances of his life and writings and to the ideological and historical context within which his ideas were disseminated and criticised. But to the methodologist, as opposed to the historian, of social science all this is immaterial. It does not matter to him if the unexpectedly contemporary flavour of Weber's writings is a matter of coincidence provided that the critical attention which they therefore invite is shown to be repaid. His concern is rather that which led Bertrand Russell, in what has been called the best book ever written by one philosopher about another, to appraise and correct the arguments of Leibniz – a concern, as Russell put it himself in his preface, 'with philosophic truth and falsehood rather than historic fact'. The justification of a critique of Weber, as of Leibniz, is what can be learnt from it. It is of value only to the degree that it helps towards the resolution of questions which have the same urgency to ourselves as they had to him.

If such a critique could truly claim to resolve all the questions which Weber sought to answer, it would constitute not simply a modest contribution to the philosophy of the social sciences but a major and even a spectacular one. It goes without saying that I make no such claim for the present essay. But I do claim that if its arguments can be vindicated it will have shown the lines along which that major contribution will one day be made. No doubt, the ultimate concerns of philosophy, as these are defined by the Kantian tradition of which Weber is a part, can, as Weber recognised, only be accommodated. They cannot be resolved, and the sociologist, whatever the strength of the metaphysical convictions by which his personal life is guided, must concede that he has no more authority to pronounce on them than the preacher or the poet. But the questions which properly fall within the methodology of social science are not inherently unanswerable in this way. It may be optimistic, but it is not merely naïve, to hope to make acknowledged progress on the topics to which Weber's notions of ideal types, understanding and value-relevance were intended as a contribution. For me, at least, the attempt to remedy their inadequacy and to correct the three significant errors which I think Weber commits has resolved a long-standing unease about the terms in which the familiar arguments over the scope and nature of the sciences of man have been framed. The test of my suggested amendment of Weber, therefore, will be whether it can do the same for others besides myself.

103

INDEX

105

Weber, Max (*cont.*)
8, 10, 23n, 30n, 71n; *Rational and Social Foundations of Music*, 8n; *Religion of China*, 7n; *Religion of India*, 7n

Winch, Peter, 21n
Windelband, Wilhelm, 12, 22n, 39
Wittgenstein, Ludwig, 21, 39n, 44n, 57, 80, 91, 98, 100